PRAISE FOR RICHARD RODRIGUEZ AND

Days of Obligation

"With *Days of Obligation*, Richard Rodriguez has nearly come full circle, right down to the prose, whose lyrical intensity stands in sharp contrast to *Hunger of Memory*'s brittle minimalism. He is a dedicated stylist, turning arguments over and over, at times cynically detached, at others disarmingly revelatory about his own conflicts. The language expands and contracts, following the contours of alienation, love, and mourning. He writes with the enthusiasm of a younger writer exploring themes he once dismissed (he was so much older when he wrote *Hunger*, he's younger now)."

—Ruben Martinez, *Los Angeles Weekly*

"A book of astonishing beauty . . . Here is a writer who can make words riot."

—Kathy Dobie, *Vogue*

"Richard Rodriguez's prose . . . is capable of crystallizing powerful sentiment into concise and lovely shapes. His sentences embrace beauty and want to resist strict narrative . . . There is no way to contain Richard Rodriguez's mind or meditations, in a space such as this. His manner is too frank, his view is too dark and sweeping, the issues he addresses are too sizable and complex to be fairly represented . . . Perhaps it's best to simply appreciate the mind capable of asking all the right questions about cultural identity, and to savor the writer who can generate a bottomless paragraph."

—James Kaufmann, *Des Moines Register*

"His book is at its most powerful when Rodriguez is stalled in his lyric misgivings. What reader can say no to suspended judgments that are hung from such bright lines of language?"

—Richard Lacayo, *Time* magazine

"Rodriguez again threatens to redefine the way we think about ethnicity, education, and religion in present-day America. And he does so in disarmingly baroque prose—poetical, nuanced, and at times heroic . . . At the slightest hint of ideology, Rodriguez retreats into poetry and irony. His aloofness is worthy of Naipaul; his vision of America echoes Ralph Ellison; and his gimlet eye reminds us of Joan Didion . . . Rodriguez's moral and aesthetic imagination guarantees that this beautiful book will linger long after the polemics in the culture wars subside. Everywhere here, one is in the presence of a superior sensibility."
—*Kirkus Reviews*

"There is something terribly moving about [Rodriguez's] dilemma, and admirable, too, as if he is the proud flag of an unknown country."
—*Mirabella*

"Unblinkered by any political agenda, looking always toward complexity and away from sentimentality, he accomplishes something truly remarkable: he rescues the word *multicultural* from the buzzword junkheap. Rodriguez's spiritual autobiography, both here and in *Hunger of Memory*, is to the late twentieth century what John Stuart Mill's autobiography was to the Victorian era."
—ALA *Booklist*

"Rodriguez's expansive view breaks through the biological confines of ethnicity into something like true humanity. It's what makes his work well worth reading."
—*The Christian Science Monitor*

"What Didion did for [California's] New York-Los Angeles axis, its Protestant, disorderly, and American sense of itself, Rodriguez has now done for California's Mexico City-Los Angeles axis, its Catholic, tragic, and Mexican sense of itself."

—Jim Wasserman, *The Fresno Bee*

"We have yet to see in Britain a writer who can explore the immigrant experience with such delicacy and power."

—*Times Educational Review* (London)

"If Caliban—the envious servant in Shakespeare's *The Tempest*, who haunts his master Prospero's library—was ever an appropriate way to label someone like Rodriguez, it isn't now. The English-speaking world is adjusting to the idea that brown-skinned writers like Derek Walcott, Toni Morrison, V. S. Naipaul, Michael Ondaatje, and Rohinton Mistry are the standard bearers of the language. Rodriguez is one of them."

—Val Ross, *The Globe and Mail* (Toronto)

"Wider in range than most self-chroniclers, Rodriguez consistently defines the intersections of personal history and larger social issues."

—Rockwell Gray, *Chicago Tribune*

"Profound and brilliant . . . This extraordinarily beautiful book . . . reaches far beyond its immediate subject to become not only one of the most exciting reads in recent memory, but a beautiful essay about all of us."

—Louise Bernikow, *Cosmopolitan*

PENGUIN BOOKS

DAYS OF OBLIGATION

Richard Rodriguez is the author of *Hunger of Memory*. He works as an editor at The Pacific News Service in San Francisco and is a contributing editor for *Harper's* and the Sunday "Opinion" section of the *Los Angeles Times*. He appears on the "MacNeil/Lehrer NewsHour" as an essayist. Mr. Rodriguez lives in San Francisco.

Days of Obligation

An Argument with My Mexican Father

Richard Rodriguez

PENGUIN BOOKS

PENGUIN BOOKS

Published by the Penguin Group

Penguin Books USA Inc., 375 Hudson Street, New York, New York 10014, U.S.A.

Penguin Books Ltd, 27 Wrights Lane, London W8 5TZ, England

Penguin Books Australia Ltd, Ringwood, Victoria, Australia

Penguin Books Canada Ltd, 10 Alcorn Avenue, Toronto, Ontario, Canada M4V 3B2

Penguin Books (N.Z.) Ltd, 182–190 Wairau Road, Auckland 10, New Zealand

Penguin Books Ltd, Registered Offices: Harmondsworth, Middlesex, England

First published in the United States of America by Viking Penguin,
a division of Penguin Books USA Inc., 1992
Published in Penguin Books 1993

1 3 5 7 9 10 8 6 4 2

THE LIBRARY OF CONGRESS HAS CATALOGUED THE HARDCOVER AS FOLLOWS:

Rodriguez, Richard.

Days of obligation: an argument with my Mexican father/by Richard Rodriguez

p. cm.

ISBN 0-670-81396-6 (hc.)

ISBN 0 14 00.9622 1 (pbk.)

1. Rodriguez, Richard. 2. Mexican Americans—California—Biography.
3. Mexican Americans—Ethnic identity. 4. Rodriguez, Richard—Journeys—Mexico.
5. Mexico—Biography. 6. Mexico—Civilization—20th century. I. Title.

F870.M5R6 1992

979.4′0046872—dc20 92—54077

Printed in the United States of America
Set in Bodoni Book
Designed by Francesca Belanger

ANN ARMISTEAD, A CALIFORNIAN

1911–1986
Santa Maria–San Francisco

Apology

Some names and biographical details
in this book have been altered.

Acknowledgments

Portions of this book have been published, in different form, in *Harper's*; *Image*; *The American Scholar*; the *Los Angeles Times Magazine*; *California*; *The New Republic*; *Time*; *To the Promised Land: Photographs by Ken Light* (Aperture Books, New York); *Frontiers: The Book of the TV Series* (BBC Books, London); *Political Passages: Journeys of Change Through Two Decades, 1968–1988*, edited by John H. Bunzel (Free Press, New York); and in the catalogue for an exhibition entitled "Visionary San Francisco," sponsored by the San Francisco Museum of Modern Art.

I am indebted, beyond repayment, to Sandy Close and to the Pacific News Service; to Franz Schurmann, Lynn O'Donnell, and Alberto Huerta, S.J., for their intellectual companionship; to my sister, Helen, for her support; and to Elizabeth Blake, who (when I found her, one day, repainting the walls of Mission San Luis Rey near Oceanside) taught me a lesson so crucial and simple about Indians in California that I was able to imagine my task.

Contents

My Parents' Village

I am on my knees, my mouth over the mouth of the toilet, waiting to heave. It comes up with a bark. All the badly pronounced Spanish words I have forced myself to sound during the day, bits and pieces of Mexico spew from my mouth, warm, half-understood, nostalgic reds and greens dangle from long strands of saliva.

I am crying from my mouth in Mexico City.

Yesterday, the nausea began. Driving through Michoacán with a television crew, I was looking for a village I had never seen. The production assistant fed a Bobby Brown tape into the car stereo.

We had been on the road since breakfast. I was looking for the kind of village my parents would have known as children, the kind they left behind.

The producer was impatient—"What about that one?"—indicating with the disinterested jerk of his head yet another church spire, yet another configuration of tile roofs in the distance.

The British Broadcasting Corporation has hired me to serve as the "presenter" for a television documentary on the United States and Mexico. A man who spent so many years with his back turned to Mexico. Now I am to introduce Mexico to a European audience.

For the last several years, I have told friends that I was writing a book about California and Mexico. That was not saying enough. I've been writing a book about comedy and tragedy. In my mind, in my life, Mexico plays the tragic part; California plays the role of America's wild child.

Or was I writing a book about competing theologies?

Josiah Royce, another Californian, another writer, became a famous Harvard professor. Royce wrote about California with disappointment from the distance of New England. Royce believed that some epic opportunity had been given California— the chance to reconcile the culture of the Catholic south and the Protestant north. California had the chance to heal the sixteenth-century tear of Europe. But the opportunity was lost. The Catholic—the Mexican—impulse was pushed back, vanquished by comedy; a Protestant conquest.

I use the word "comedy" here as the Greeks used it, with utmost seriousness, to suggest a world where youth is not a fruitless metaphor; where it is possible to start anew; where it is possible to escape the rivalries of the Capulets and the McCoys; where young women can disprove the adages of grandmothers.

The comedy of California was constructed on a Protestant faith in individualism. Whereas Mexico knew tragedy.

My Mexican father, as his father before him, believed that old men know more than young men; that life will break your heart; that death finally is the vantage point from which a life must be seen.

I think now that Mexico has been the happier place for being a country of tragedy. Tragic cultures serve up better food than optimistic cultures; tragic cultures have sweeter children, more opulent funerals. In tragic cultures, one does not bear the solitary burden of optimism. California is such a sad place, really—a state where children run away from parents, a state of pale beer, and young old women, and divorced husbands living alone in condos. But at a time when Californians are driven to despair by the relentless optimism of their state, I can only marvel at the comic achievement of the place, California's defiance of history, the defiance of ancestors.

Something hopeful was created in California through the century of its Protestant settlement. People believed that in California they could begin new lives. New generations of immigrants continue to arrive in California, not a few of them from Mexico, hoping to cash in on comedy.

It is still possible in California to change your name, change your sex, get a divorce, become a movie star. My Mexican parents live in a California house with four telephones, three televisions, and several empty bedrooms.

How could California ever reconcile comedy and tragedy? How could there not have been a divorce between Mexico and California in the nineteenth century?

The youth of my life was defined by Protestant optimism. Now that I am middle-aged, I incline more toward the Mexican point of view, though some part of me continues to resist the cynical conclusions of Mexico.

Which leaves me with at least a literary problem to start with: How shall I present the argument between comedy and tragedy, this tension that describes my life? Shall I start with the boy's chapter, then move toward more "mature" tragic conclusions? But that would underplay the boy's wisdom. The middle-aged man would simply lord over the matter.

No, I will present this life in reverse. After all, the journey my parents took from Mexico to America was a journey from an

Introduction

ancient culture to a youthful one—backward in time. In their path I similarly move, if only to honor their passage to California, and because I believe the best resolution to the debate between comedy and tragedy is irresolution, since both sides can claim wisdom.

Yesterday, around noontime, I recognized it. We were driving along the two-lane Mexican highway and there it was—just off to the right, past a grove of eucalyptus—the village of childhood imagining.

The production assistant radioed the other cars in our caravan to follow. We turned down a muddy road.

The village was constructed around a central square. Passage toward the center was narrow; just room enough for a van filled with our television equipment to pass. Most of the doors of the village were open. We saw few people about; those few more curious than friendly, more Indian than mestizo.

This is perfect, I kept saying from the back seat, perfect.

I could imagine my father as a boy, dreaming of running away from just such a village. I could see my mother's paradise—she of the sausage curls, the lampshade dress.

Ahead I spied a church on the south side of the square. There was a crumbling fountain. Also a crowd of women in dark shawls. Market day? All the better.

The church bell was tolling. I don't wear a watch. It must be noon.

And then I saw the reason for the crowd in the plaza—a tiny coffin was being lifted from the bed of a truck. At the same moment, people at the edge of the crowd turned toward our noisy procession.

Bobby Brown panted Unh-oh-ahhhhhhhh from our rolled-down windows.

A village idiot—a cripple—hobbled toward us, his face contorted into what was either a grin or a grimace, his finger pressed against his lips.

Silencio. Silencio.

"Turn off the music," the producer shouted.

The production assistant radioed the rest of the convoy: Back up, back up.

There was no room to turn.

The van, the two cars shifted into reverse. Then my stomach began to churn.

My vision of the Mexican village—yellow doors, wet gutters, children with preternaturally large eyes—floated backward. The crowd of mourners in the village square became smaller and smaller and smaller.

Days of Obligation

CHAPTER ONE

India

At sunrise the next day, the time the Indians appointed, they came according to their promise, and brought us a large quantity of fish with certain roots. . . . They sent their women and children to look at us. . . .

Álvar Núñez Cabeza de Vaca

I used to stare at the Indian in the mirror. The wide nostrils, the thick lips. Starring Paul Muni as Benito Juárez. Such a long face—such a long nose—sculpted by indifferent, blunt thumbs, and of such common clay. No one in my family had a face as dark or as Indian as mine. My face could not portray the ambition I brought to it. What could the United States of America say to me? I remember reading the ponderous conclusion of the Kerner Report in the sixties: two Americas, one white, one black—the prophecy of an eclipse too simple to account for the complexity of my face.

1

Mestizo in Mexican Spanish means mixed, confused. Clotted with Indian, thinned by Spanish spume.

What could Mexico say to me?

Mexican philosophers powwow in their tony journals about Indian "fatalism" and "Whither Mexico?" *El fatalismo del indio* is an important Mexican philosophical theme; the phrase is trusted to conjure the quality of Indian passivity as well as to initiate debate about Mexico's reluctant progress toward modernization. Mexicans imagine their Indian part as deadweight: the Indian stunned by modernity; so overwhelmed by the loss of what is genuine to him—his language, his religion—that he sits weeping like a medieval lady at the crossroads; or else he resorts to occult powers and superstitions, choosing to consort with death because the purpose of the world has passed him by.

One night in Mexico City I ventured from my hotel to a distant *colonia* to visit my aunt, my father's only sister. But she was not there. She had moved. For the past several years she has moved, this woman of eighty-odd years, from one of her children to another. She takes with her only her papers and books—she is a poetess—and an upright piano painted blue. My aunt writes love poems to her dead husband, Juan—keeping Juan up to date, while rewatering her loss. Last year she sent me her *obras completas*, an inch-thick block of bound onionskin. And with her poems she sent me a list of names, a genealogy braiding two centuries, two continents, to a common origin: eighteenth-century Salamanca. No explanation is attached to the list. Its implication is nonetheless clear. We are—my father's family is (despite the evidence of my face)—of Europe. We are not Indian.

On the other hand, a Berkeley undergraduate approached me one day, creeping up as if I were a stone totem to say, "God, it must be cool to be related to Aztecs."

• • •

India

I sat down next to the journalist from Pakistan—the guest of honor. He had been making a tour of the United States under the auspices of the U.S. State Department. Nearing the end of his journey now, he was having dinner with several of us, American journalists, at a Chinese restaurant in San Francisco. He said he'd seen pretty much all he wanted to see in America. His wife, however, had asked him to bring back some American Indian handicrafts. Blankets. Beaded stuff. He'd looked everywhere.

The table was momentarily captured by the novelty of his dilemma. You can't touch the stuff nowadays, somebody said. So rare, so expensive. Somebody else knew of a shop up on Sacramento Street that sells authentic Santa Fe. Several others remembered a store in Chinatown where moccasins, belts—"the works"—were to be found. All manufactured in Taiwan.

The Pakistani journalist looked incredulous. His dream of America had been shaped by American export-Westerns. Cowboys and Indians are yin and yang of America. He had seen men dressed like cowboys on this trip. But (turning to me): Where are the Indians?

(Two Indians staring at one another. One asks where are all the Indians, the other shrugs.)

■　■　■

I grew up in Sacramento thinking of Indians as people who had disappeared. I was a Mexican in California; I would no more have thought of myself as an Aztec in California than you might imagine yourself a Viking or a Bantu. Mrs. Ferrucci up the block used to call my family "Spanish." We knew she intended to ennoble us by that designation. We also knew she was ignorant.

I was ignorant.

In America the Indian is relegated to the obligatory first chapter—the "Once Great Nation" chapter—after which the Indian is cleared away as easily as brush, using a very sharp rhetorical tool called an "alas." Thereafter, the Indian reappears only as a stunned remnant—Ishi, or the hundred-year-old hag blowing out her birthday candle at a rest home in Tucson; or the teenager drunk on his ass in Plaza Park.

Here they come down Broadway in the Fourth of July parades of my childhood—middle-aged men wearing glasses, beating their tom-toms; Hey-ya-ya-yah; Hey-ya-ya-yah. They wore Bermuda shorts under their loincloths. High-school kids could never refrain from the answering Woo-woo-woo, stopping their mouths with the palms of their hands.

In the 1960s, Indians began to name themselves Native Americans, recalling themselves to life. That self-designation underestimated the ruthless idea Puritans had superimposed upon the landscape. America is an idea to which natives are inimical. The Indian represented permanence and continuity to Americans who were determined to call this country new. Indians must be ghosts.

I collected conflicting evidence concerning Mexico, it's true, but I never felt myself the remnant of anything. Mexican magazines arrived in our mailbox from Mexico City; showed pedestrians strolling wide ocher boulevards beneath trees with lime-green leaves. My past was at least this coherent: Mexico was a real place with plenty of people walking around in it. My parents had come from somewhere that went on without them.

When I was a graduate student at Berkeley, teaching remedial English, there were a few American Indians in my classroom. They were unlike any other "minority students" in the classes I taught. The Indians drifted in and out. When I summoned them to my office, they came and sat while I did all the talking.

I remember one tall man particularly, a near-somnambulist, beautiful in an off-putting way, but interesting, too, because I never saw him without the current issue of *The New York Review of Books* under his arm, which I took as an advertisement of ambition. He eschewed my class for weeks at a time. Then one morning I saw him in a café on Telegraph Avenue, across from Cody's. I did not fancy myself Sidney Poitier, but I was interested in this moody brave's lack of interest in me, for one, and then *The New York Review*.

Do you mind if I sit here?

Nothing.

Blah, Blah, Blah . . . *N. Y. R. B. ?*—entirely on my part— until, when I got up to leave:

"You're not Indian, you're Mexican," he said. "You wouldn't understand."

He meant I was cut. Diluted.

Understand what?

He meant I was not an Indian in America. He meant he was an enemy of the history that had otherwise created me. And he was right, I didn't understand. I took his diffidence for chauvinism. I read his chauvinism as arrogance. He didn't see the Indian in my face? I saw his face—his refusal to consort with the living—as the face of a dead man.

As the landscape goes, so goes the Indian? In the public-service TV commercial, the Indian sheds a tear at the sight of an America polluted beyond his recognition. Indian memory has become the measure against which America gauges corrupting history when it suits us. Gitchigoomeism—the habit of placing the Indian outside history—is a white sentimentality that relegates the Indian to death.

An obituary from *The New York Times* (September 1989— dateline Alaska): An oil freighter has spilled its load along the Alaskan coast. There is a billion-dollar cleanup, bringing jobs and dollars to Indian villages.

> The modern world has been closing in on English Bay
> . . . with glacial slowness. The oil spill and the resulting
> sea of money have accelerated the process, so that
> English Bay now seems caught on the cusp of history.

The omniscient reporter from *The New York Times* takes it upon himself to regret history on behalf of the Indians.

> Instead of hanging salmon to dry this month, as Aleut
> natives have done for centuries . . . John Kvasnikoff
> was putting up a three thousand dollar television sat-
> ellite dish on the bluff next to his home above the sea.

The reporter from *The New York Times* knows the price modernity will exact from an Indian who wants to plug himself in. Mind you, the reporter is confident of his own role in history, his freedom to lug a word processor to some remote Alaskan village. About the reporter's journey, *The New York Times* is not censorious. But let the Indian drop one bead from custom, or let his son straddle a snowmobile—as he does in the photo accompanying the article—and *The New York Times* cries Boo-hoo-hoo yah-yah-yah.

Thus does the Indian become the mascot of an international ecology movement. The industrial countries of the world romanticize the Indian who no longer exists, ignoring the Indian who does—the Indian who is poised to chop down his rain forest, for example. Or the Indian who reads *The New York Times*.

Once more in San Francisco: I flattered myself that the woman staring at me all evening "knew my work." I considered myself an active agent, in other words. But, after several passes around the buffet, the woman cornered me to say she recognized me as an "ancient soul."

Do I lure or am I just minding my own business?

Is it the nature of Indians—not verifiable in nature, of course, but in the European description of Indians—that we wait around to be "discovered"?

Europe discovers. India beckons. Isn't that so? India sits atop her lily pad through centuries, lost in contemplation of the horizon. And, from time to time, India is discovered.

In the fifteenth century, sailing Spaniards were acting according to scientific conjecture as to the nature and as to the shape of the world. Most thinking men in Europe at the time of Columbus believed the world to be round. The voyage of Columbus was the test of a theory believed to be true. Brave, yes, but pedantic therefore.

The Indian is forever implicated in the roundness of the world. America was the false India, the mistaken India, and yet veritable India, for all that—India—the clasp, the coupling mystery at the end of quest.

This is as true today as of yore. Where do the Beatles go when the world is too much with them? Where does Jerry Brown seek the fat farm of his soul? India, man, India!

India waits.

India has all the answers beneath her passive face or behind her veil or between her legs. The European has only questions, questions that are assertions turned inside out, questions that can only be answered by sailing toward the abysmal horizon.

The lusty Europeans wanted the shortest answers. They knew what they wanted. They wanted spices, pagodas, gold.

Had the world been flat, had the European sought the unknown, then the European would have been as great a victor over history as he has portrayed himself to be. The European would have outdistanced history—even theology—if he could have arrived at the shore of some prelapsarian state. If the world had been flat, then the European could have traveled outward toward innocence.

But the world was round. The entrance into the Indies was a reunion of peoples. The Indian awaited the long-separated European, the inevitable European, as the approaching horizon.

Though perhaps, too, there was some demiurge felt by the human race of the fifteenth century to heal itself, to make itself whole? Certainly, in retrospect, there was some inevitability to the Catholic venture. If the world was round, continuous, then so, too, were peoples?

According to the European version—the stag version—of the pageant of the New World, the Indian must play a passive role. Europe has been accustomed to play the swaggart in history—Europe striding through the Americas, overturning temples, spilling language, spilling seed, spilling blood.

And wasn't the Indian the female, the passive, the waiting aspect to the theorem—lewd and promiscuous in her embrace as she is indolent betimes?

Charles Macomb Flandrau, a native of St. Paul, Minnesota, wrote a book called *Viva Mexico!* in 1908, wherein he described the Mexican Indian as "incorrigibly plump. One never ceases to marvel at the superhuman strength existing beneath the pretty and effeminate modeling of their arms and legs and backs. . . . The legs of an American 'strong man' look usually like an anatomical chart, but the legs of the most powerful Totonac Indian —and the power of many of them is beyond belief—would serve admirably as one of those idealized extremities on which women's hosiery is displayed in shop windows."

In Western Civilization histories, the little honeymoon joke Europe tells on itself is of mistaking America for the extremities of India. But India was perhaps not so much a misnomer as was "discoverer" or "conquistador."

Earliest snapshots of Indians brought back to Europe were of naked little woodcuts, arms akimbo, resembling Erasmus, or of grandees in capes and feathered tiaras, courtiers of an Egyptified palace of nature. In European museums, she is idle, recumbent at the base of a silver pineapple tree or the pedestal of the Dresden urn or the Sèvres tureen—the muse of European adventure, at once wanderlust and bounty.

Many tribes of Indians were prescient enough, preserved memory enough, or were lonesome enough to predict the coming of a pale stranger from across the sea, a messianic twin of completing memory or skill.

None of this could the watery Europeans have known as they marveled at the sight of approaching land. Filled with the arrogance of discovery, the Europeans were not predisposed to imagine that they were being watched, awaited.

■ ■ ■

That friend of mine at Oxford loses patience whenever I describe my face as mestizo. Look at my face. What do you see?

An Indian, he says.

Mestizo, I correct.

Mestizo, mestizo, he says.

Listen, he says. I went back to my mother's village in Mexico last summer and there was nothing mestizo about it. Dust, dogs, and Indians. People there don't even speak Spanish.

So I ask my friend at Oxford what it means to him to be an Indian.

He hesitates. My friend has recently been taken up as amusing by a bunch of rich Pakistanis in London. But, facing me, he is vexed and in earnest. He describes a lonely search among his family for evidence of Indian-ness. He thinks he has found it in his mother; watching his mother in her garden.

Does she plant corn by the light of the moon?

She seems to have some relationship with the earth, he says quietly.

So there it is. The mystical tie to nature. How else to think of the Indian except in terms of some druidical green thumb? No one says of an English matron in her rose garden that she is behaving like a Celt. Because the Indian has no history—that is, because history books are the province of the descendants of Europeans—the Indian seems only to belong to the party of the first part, the first chapter. So that is where the son expects to find his mother, Daughter of the Moon.

Let's talk about something else. Let's talk about London. The last time I was in London, I was walking toward an early evening at the Queen's Theatre when I passed that Christopher Wren church near Fortnum & Mason. The church was lit; I decided to stop, to savor the spectacle of what I expected would be a few Pymish men and women rolled into balls of fur at evensong. Imagine my surprise that the congregation was young—dressed in army fatigues and Laura Ashley. Within the chancel, cross-legged on a dais, was a South American shaman.

Now, who is the truer Indian in this picture? Me . . . me on my way to the Queen's Theatre? Or that guy on the altar with a Ph.D. in death?

■ ■ ■

We have hurled—like starlings, like Goths—through the castle of European memory. Our reflections have glanced upon the golden coach that carried the Emperor Maximilian through the streets of Mexico City, thence onward through the sludge of a hundred varnished paintings.

I have come at last to Mexico, the country of my parents' birth. I do not expect to find anything that pertains to me.

We have strained the rouge cordon at the thresholds of imperial apartments; seen chairs low enough for dwarfs, commodious enough for angels.

We have imagined the Empress Carlota standing in the shadows of an afternoon; we have followed her gaze down the Paseo de la Reforma toward the distant city. The Paseo was a nostalgic allusion to the Champs-Elysées, we learn, which Maximilian recreated for his tempestuous, crowlike bride.

Come this way, please. . . .

European memory is not to be the point of our excursion. Señor Fuentes, our tour director, is already beginning to descend the hill from Chapultepec Castle. What the American credit-card company calls our "orientation tour" of Mexico City had started late and so Señor Fuentes has been forced, regrettably,

". . . This way, please . . ."

to rush. Señor Fuentes is consumed with contrition for time wasted this morning. He intends to uphold his schedule, as a way of upholding Mexico, against our expectation.

We had gathered at the appointed time at the limousine entrance to our hotel, beneath the banner welcoming contestants to the Señorita Mexico pageant. We—Japanese, Germans, Americans—were waiting promptly at nine. There was no bus. And as we waited, the Señorita Mexico contestants arrived. Drivers leaned into their cabs to pull out long-legged señoritas. The drivers then balanced the señoritas onto stiletto heels (the driveway was cobbled) before they passed the señoritas, *en pointe,* to the waiting arms of officials.

Mexican men, meanwhile—doormen, bellhops, window washers, hotel guests—stopped dead in their tracks, wounded by the scent and spectacle of so many blond señoritas. The Mexican men assumed fierce expressions, nostrils flared, brows knit. Such expressions are masks—the men intend to convey their adoration of prey—as thoroughly ritualized as the smiles of beauty queens.

By now we can see the point of our excursion beyond the parched trees of Chapultepec Park—the Museo Nacional de Antropología—which is an air-conditioned repository for the artifacts of the Indian civilizations of Meso-America, the finest anthropological museum in the world.

"There will not be time to see everything," Señor Fuentes warns as he ushers us into the grand salon, our first experience of the suffocating debris of The Ancients. Señor Fuentes wants us in and out of here by noon.

Whereas the United States traditionally has rejoiced at the delivery of its landscape from "savagery," Mexico has taken its national identity only from the Indian, the mother. Mexico measures all cultural bastardy against the Indian; equates civilization with India—Indian kingdoms of a golden age; cities as fabulous as Alexandria or Benares or Constantinople; a court as hairless, as subtle as the Pekingese. Mexico equates barbarism with Europe—beardedness—with Spain.

It is curious, therefore, that both modern nations should similarly apostrophize the Indian, relegate the Indian to the past.

Come this way, please. Mrs. . . . Ah . . . this way, please.

Señor Fuentes wears an avocado-green sports coat with gold buttons. He is short. He is rather elegant, with a fine small head, small hands, small feet; with his two rows of fine small teeth like a nutcracker's teeth, with which he curtails consonants as cleanly as bitten thread. Señor Fuentes is brittle, he is watchful, he is ironic, he is metropolitan; his wit is quotational, literary, wasted on Mrs. Ah.

He is not our equal. His demeanor says he is not our equal. We mistake his condescension for humility. He will not eat when we eat. He will not spend when we shop. He will not have done with Mexico when we have done with Mexico.

Señor Fuentes is impatient with us, for we have paused momentarily outside the museum to consider the misfortune of an adolescent mother who holds her crying baby out to us. Several of us confer among ourselves in an attempt to place a peso value on the woman's situation. We do not ask for the advice of Señor Fuentes.

For we, in turn, are impatient with Señor Fuentes. We are in a bad mood. The air conditioning on our "fully air-conditioned coach" is nonexistent. We have a headache. Nor is the city air any relief, but it is brown, fungal, farted.

Señor Fuentes is a mystery to us, for there is no American equivalent to him; for there is no American equivalent to the subtleties he is paid to describe to us.

Mexico will not raise a public monument to Hernán Cortés, for example, the father of Mexico—the rapist. In the Diego Rivera murals in the presidential palace, the Aztec city of Tenochtitlán is rendered—its blood temples and blood canals—as haughty as Troy, as vulnerable as Pompeii. Any suggestion of the complicity of other tribes of Indians in overthrowing the Aztec empire is painted over. Spaniards appear on the horizons of Arcadia as syphilitic brigands and demon-eyed priests.

The Spaniard entered the Indian by entering her city—the floating city—first as a suitor, ceremoniously; later by force. How should Mexico honor the rape?

In New England the European and the Indian drew apart to regard each other with suspicion over centuries. Miscegenation was a sin against Protestant individualism. In Mexico the European and the Indian consorted. The ravishment of fabulous Tenochtitlán ended in a marriage of blood—a "cosmic race," the Mexican philosopher José Vasconcelos has called it.

Mexico's tragedy is that she has no political idea of herself as rich as her blood.

The rhetoric of Señor Fuentes, like the murals of Diego Rivera, resorts often to the dream of India—to Tenochtitlán, the capital of the world before conquest. "Preconquest" in the Mexican political lexicon is tantamount to "prelapsarian" in the Judeo-

Christian scheme, and hearkens to a time Mexico feels herself to have been whole, a time before the Indian was separated from India by the serpent Spain.

Three centuries after Cortés, Mexico declared herself independent of Spain. If Mexico would have no yoke, then Mexico would have no crown, then Mexico would have no father. The denial of Spain has persisted into our century.

The priest and the landowner yet serve Señor Fuentes as symbols of the hated Spanish order. Though, in private, Mexico is Catholic; Mexican mothers may wish for light-skinned children. Touch blond hair and good luck will be yours.

In private, in Mexican Spanish, *indio* is a seller of Chiclets, a sidewalk squatter. *Indio* means backward or lazy or lower-class. In the eyes of the world, Mexico raises a magnificent museum of anthropology—the finest in the world—to honor the Indian mother.

In the nave of the National Cathedral, we notice the floor slopes dramatically. "The cathedral is sinking," Señor Fuentes explains as a hooded figure approaches our group from behind a column. She is an Indian woman; she wears a blue stole; her hands are cupped, beseeching; tear marks ream her cheeks. In Spanish, Señor Fuentes forbids this apparition: "Go ask *padrecito* to pry some gold off the altar for you."

"Mexico City is built upon swamp," Señor Fuentes resumes in English. "Therefore, the cathedral is sinking." But it is clear that Señor Fuentes believes the sinkage is due to the oppressive weight of Spanish Catholicism, its masses of gold, its volumes of deluded suspiration.

Mexican political life can only seem Panglossian when you consider an anti-Catholic government of an overwhelmingly Catholic population. Mexico is famous for politicians descended from Masonic fathers and Catholic mothers. Señor Fuentes himself is less a Spaniard, less an Indian, perhaps, than an embittered eighteenth-century man, clinging to the witty knees of Voltaire against the chaos of twentieth-century Mexico.

Mexico blamed the ruin of the nineteenth century on the foreigner, and with reason. Once emptied of Spain, the palace of Mexico became the dollhouse of France. Mexico was overrun by imperial armies. The greed of Europe met the Manifest Destiny of the United States in Mexico. Austria sent an archduke to marry Mexico with full panoply of candles and bishops. The U.S. reached under Mexico's skirt every chance he got.

"Poor Mexico, so far from God, so close to the United States."

Señor Fuentes dutifully attributes the mot to Porfirio Díaz, the Mexican president who sold more of Mexico to foreign interests than any other president. It was against the regime of Porfirio Díaz that Mexicans rebelled in the early decades of this century. Mexico prefers to call its civil war a "revolution."

Mexico for Mexicans!

The Revolution did not accomplish a union of Mexicans. The Revolution did not accomplish a restoration of Mexicans to their landscape. The dust of the Revolution parted to reveal—not India—but Marx *ex machina*, the Institutional Revolutionary Party, the PRI—a political machine appropriate to the age of steam. The Institutional Revolutionary Party, as its name implies, was designed to reconcile institutional pragmatism with revolutionary rhetoric. And the PRI worked for a time, because it gave Mexico what Mexico most needed, the stability of compromise.

The PRI appears everywhere in Mexico—a slogan on the wall, the politician impersonating a journalist on the evening news, the professor at his podium. The PRI is in its way as much a Mexican institution as the Virgin of Guadalupe.

Now Mexicans speak of the government as something imposed upon them, and they are the victims of it. But the political failure of Mexico must be counted a failure of Mexicans. Whom now shall Señor Fuentes blame for a twentieth century that has become synonymous with corruption?

Well, as long as you stay out of the way of the police no one will bother you, is conventional Mexican wisdom, and Mexico continues to live her daily life. In the capital, the air is the color of the buildings of Siena. Telephone connections are an aspect of the will of God. Mexicans drive on the sidewalks. A man on the street corner seizes the opportunity of stalled traffic to earn his living as a fire-eater. His ten children pass among the cars and among the honking horns to collect small coins.

Thank you. Thank you very much. A pleasure, Mrs. . . . Ah. Thank you very much.

Señor Fuentes bids each farewell. He accepts tips within a handshake. He bows slightly. We have no complaint with Señor Fuentes, after all. The bus was not his fault. Mexico City is not his fault. And Señor Fuentes will return to his unimaginable Mexico and we will return to our rooms to take aspirin and to initiate long-distance telephone calls. Señor Fuentes will remove his avocado-green coat and, having divested, Señor Fuentes will in some fashion partake of what he has successfully kept from us all day, which is the life and the drinking water of Mexico.

■ ■ ■

The Virgin of Guadalupe symbolizes the entire coherence of Mexico, body and soul. You will not find the story of the Virgin within hidebound secular histories of Mexico—nor indeed within the credulous repertoire of Señor Fuentes—and the omission renders the history of Mexico incomprehensible.

One recent afternoon, within the winy bell jar of a very late lunch, I told the story of the Virgin of Guadalupe to Lynn, a sophisticated twentieth-century woman. The history of Mexico, I promised her, is neither mundane nor masculine, but it is a

16

miracle play with trapdoors and sequins and jokes on the living.

In the sixteenth century, when Indians were demoralized by the routing of their gods, when millions of Indians were dying from the plague of Europe, the Virgin Mary appeared pacing on a hillside to an Indian peasant named Juan Diego—his Christian name, for Juan was a convert. It was December 1531.

On his way to mass, Juan passed the hill called Tepayac . . .

Just as the East was beginning to kindle
To dawn. He heard there a cloud
Of birdsong bursting overhead
Of whistles and flutes and beating wings
—Now here, now there—
A mantle of chuckles and berries and rain
That rocked through the sky like the great Spanish bell
In Mexico City;
At the top of the hill there shone a light
And the light called out a name to him
With a lady's voice.
Juan, Juan,
The Lady-light called.
Juan crossed himself, he fell to his knees,
He covered his eyes and prepared to be blinded.

He could see through his hands that covered his face
As the sun rose up from behind her cape,
That the poor light of day
Was no match for this Lady, but broke upon her
Like a waterfall,
A rain of rings.
She wore a gown the color of dawn.
Her hair was braided with ribbons and flowers
And tiny tinkling silver bells. Her mantle was sheer
And bright as rain and embroidered with thousands

of twinkling stars.
A clap before curtains, like waking from sleep;
Then a human face,
A mother's smile;
Her complexion as red as cinnamon bark;
Cheeks as brown as pérsimmon.

Her eyes were her voice,
As modest and shy as a pair of doves
In the eaves of her brow. Her voice was
Like listening. This lady spoke
In soft Nahuatl, the Aztec tongue
(As different from Spanish
As some other season of weather,
As doves in the boughs of a summer tree
Are different from crows in a wheeling wind,
Who scatter destruction and
Caw caw caw caw)—
Nahuatl like rain, like water flowing, like drips in a
cavern,
Or glistening thaw,
Like breath through a flute,
With many stops and plops and sighs . . .

Peering through the grille of her cigarette smoke, Lynn heard and she seemed to approve the story.

At the Virgin's behest, this Prufrock Indian must go several times to the bishop of Mexico City. He must ask that a chapel be built on Tepayac where his discovered Lady may share in the sorrows of her people. Juan Diego's visits to the Spanish bishop parody the conversion of the Indians by the Spaniards. The bishop is skeptical.

The bishop wants proof.

18

India

The Virgin tells Juan Diego to climb the hill and gather a sheaf of roses as proof for the bishop--Castilian roses—impossible in Mexico in December of 1531. Juan carries the roses in the folds of his cloak, a pregnant messenger. Upon entering the bishop's presence, Juan parts his cloak, the roses tumble; the bishop falls to his knees.

In the end—with crumpled napkins, torn carbons, the bitter dregs of coffee—Lynn gave the story over to the Spaniards.

The legend concludes with a concession to humanity—proof more durable than roses—the imprint of the Virgin's image upon the cloak of Juan Diego . . .

A Spanish trick, Lynn said. A recruitment poster for the new religion, no more, she said (though sadly). An itinerant diva with a costume trunk. Birgit Nilsson as Aïda.

Why do we assume Spain made up the story?

The importance of the story is that Indians believed it. The jokes, the vaudeville, the relegation of the Spanish bishop to the role of comic adversary, the Virgin's chosen cavalier, and especially the brown-faced Mary—all elements spoke directly to Indians.

The result of the apparition and of the miraculous image of the Lady remaining upon the cloak of Juan Diego was a mass conversion of Indians to Catholicism.

The image of Our Lady of Guadalupe (privately, affectionately, Mexicans call her La Morenita—Little Darkling) has become the unofficial, the private flag of Mexicans. Unique possession of her image is a more wonderful election to Mexicans than any political call to nationhood. Perhaps Mexico's tragedy in our century, perhaps Mexico's abiding grace thus far, is that she has no political idea of herself as compelling as her icon.

The Virgin appears everywhere in Mexico. On dashboards and

on calendars, on playing cards, on lampshades and cigar boxes; within the loneliness and tattooed upon the very skins of Mexicans.

Nor is the image of Guadalupe a diminishing mirage of the sixteenth century, but she has become more vivid with time, developing in her replication from earthy shades of melon and musk to bubble-gum pink, Windex blue, to achieve the hard, literal focus of holy cards or baseball cards; of Krishna or St. Jude or the Atlanta Braves.

Mexico City stands as the last living medieval capital of the world. Mexico is the creation of a Spanish Catholicism that attempted to draw continents together as one flesh. The success of Spanish Catholicism in Mexico resulted in a kind of proof—a profound concession to humanity: the *mestizaje*.

What joke on the living? Lynn said.

The joke is that Spain arrived with missionary zeal at the shores of contemplation. But Spain had no idea of the absorbent strength of Indian spirituality.

By the waters of baptism, the active European was entirely absorbed within the contemplation of the Indian. The faith that Europe imposed in the sixteenth century was, by virtue of the Guadalupe, embraced by the Indian. Catholicism has become an Indian religion. By the twenty-first century, the locus of the Catholic Church, by virtue of numbers, will be Latin America, by which time Catholicism itself will have assumed the aspect of the Virgin of Guadalupe.

Brown skin.

■ ■ ■

Time magazine dropped through the chute of my mailbox a few years ago with a cover story on Mexico entitled "The Population Curse." From the vantage point of Sixth Avenue, the editors of Time-Life peer down into the basin of Mexico City—like peering down into the skull of a pumpkin—to contemplate the nightmare of fecundity, the tangled mass of slime and hair and seed.

America sees death in all that life; sees rot. Life—not illness and poverty; not death—life becomes the curse of Mexico City in the opinion of *Time* magazine.

For a long time I had my own fear of Mexico, an American fear. Mexico's history was death. Her stature was tragedy. A race of people that looked like me had disappeared.

I had a dream about Mexico City, a conquistador's dream. I was lost and late and twisted in my sheet. I dreamed streets narrower than they actually are—narrow as old Jerusalem. I dreamed sheets, entanglements, bunting, hanging larvaelike from open windows, distended from balconies and from lines thrown over the streets. These streets were not empty streets. I was among a crowd. The crowd was not a carnival crowd. This crowd was purposeful and ordinary, welling up from subways, ascending from stairwells. And then the dream followed the course of all my dreams. I must find the airport—the American solution—I must somehow escape, fly over.

Each face looked like mine. But no one looked at me.

I have come at last to Mexico, to the place of my parents' birth. I have come under the protection of an American credit-card company. I have canceled this trip three times.

As the plane descends into the basin of Mexico City, I brace myself for some confrontation with death, with India, with confusion of purpose that I do not know how to master.

Do you speak Spanish? the driver asks in English.

Andrés, the driver employed by my hotel, is in his forties. He lives in the Colonia Roma, near the airport. There is nothing about the city he does not know. This is his city and he is its memory.

Andrés's car is a dark-blue Buick—about 1975. Windows slide

up and down at the touch of his finger. There is the smell of disinfectant in Andrés's car, as there is in every bus or limousine or taxi I've ridden in Mexico—the smell of the glycerine crystals in urinals. Dangling from Andrés's rearview mirror is the other appliance common to all public conveyance in Mexico—a rosary.

Andrés is a man of the world, a man, like other working-class Mexican men, eager for the world. He speaks two languages. He knows several cities. He has been to the United States. His brother lives there still.

In the annals of the famous European discoverers there is invariably an Indian guide, a translator—willing or not—to facilitate, to preserve Europe's stride. These seem to have become fluent in pallor before Europe learned anything of them. How is that possible?

The most famous guide in Mexican history is also the most reviled by Mexican histories—the villainess Marina—"La Malinche." Marina became the lover of Cortés. So, of course, Mexicans say she betrayed India for Europe. In the end, she was herself betrayed, left behind when Cortés repaired to his Spanish wife.

Nonetheless, Marina's treachery anticipates the epic marriage of Mexico. La Malinche prefigures, as well, the other, the beloved female aspect of Mexico, the Virgin of Guadalupe.

Because Marina was the seducer of Spain, she challenges the boast Europe has always told about India.

I assure you Mexico has an Indian point of view as well, a female point of view:

I opened my little eye and the Spaniard disappeared.

Imagine a dark pool; the Spaniard dissolved; the surface triumphantly smooth.

My eye!

The spectacle of the Spaniard on the horizon, vainglorious—

the shiny surfaces, clanks of metal; the horses, the muskets, the jingling bits.

Cannot you imagine me curious? Didn't I draw near?

European vocabularies do not have a silence rich enough to describe the force within Indian contemplation. Only Shakespeare understood that Indians have eyes. Shakespeare saw Caliban eyeing his master's books—well, why not his master as well? The same dumb lust.

WHAT DAT? is a question philosophers ask. And Indians.

Shakespeare's comedy, of course, resolves itself to the European's applause. The play that Shakespeare did not write is Mexico City.

Now the great city swells under the moon; seems, now, to breathe of itself—the largest city in the world—a Globe, kind Will, not of your devising, not under your control.

The superstition persists in European travel literature that Indian Christianity is the thinnest veneer covering an ulterior altar. But there is a possibility still more frightening to the European imagination, so frightening that in five hundred years such a possibility has scarcely found utterance.

What if the Indian were converted?

The Indian eye becomes a portal through which the entire pageant of European civilization has already passed; turned inside out. Then the baroque is an Indian conceit. The colonial arcade is an Indian detail.

Look once more at the city from La Malinche's point of view. Mexico is littered with the shells and skulls of Spain, cathedrals, poems, and the limbs of orange trees. But everywhere you look in this great museum of Spain you see living Indians.

Where are the *conquistadores*?

Postcolonial Europe expresses pity or guilt behind its sleeve, pities the Indian the loss of her gods or her tongue. But let the

Indian speak for herself. Spanish is now an Indian language. Mexico City has become the metropolitan see of the Spanish-speaking world. In something like the way New York won English from London after World War I, Mexico City has captured Spanish.

The Indian stands in the same relationship to modernity as she did to Spain—willing to marry, to breed, to disappear in order to ensure her inclusion in time; refusing to absent herself from the future. The Indian has chosen to survive, to consort with the living, to live in the city, to crawl on her hands and knees, if need be, to Mexico City or L.A.

I take it as an Indian achievement that I am alive, that I am Catholic, that I speak English, that I am an American. My life began, it did not end, in the sixteenth century.

The idea occurs to me on a weekday morning, at a crowded intersection in Mexico City: Europe's lie. Here I am in the capital of death. Life surges about me; wells up from subways, wave upon wave; descends from stairwells. Everywhere I look. Babies. Traffic. Food. Beggars. Life. Life coming upon me like sunstroke.

Each face looks like mine. No one looks at me.

Where, then, is the famous conquistador?

We have eaten him, the crowd tells me, *we have eaten him with our eyes*.

I run to the mirror to see if this is true.

It is true.

In the distance, at its depths, Mexico City stands as the prophetic example. Mexico City is modern in ways that "multiracial," ethnically "diverse" New York City is not yet. Mexico City is centuries more modern than racially "pure," provincial Tokyo. Nothing to do with computers or skyscrapers.

Mexico City is the capital of modernity, for in the sixteenth century, under the tutelage of a curious Indian whore, under the patronage of the Queen of Heaven, Mexico initiated the task of the twenty-first century—the renewal of the old, the known world, through miscegenation. Mexico carries the idea of a round world to its biological conclusion.

■　■　■

For a time when he was young, Andrés, my driver, worked in Alpine County in northern California.

And then he worked at a Lake Tahoe resort. He remembers the snow. He remembers the weekends when blond California girls would arrive in their ski suits and sunglasses. Andrés worked at the top of a ski lift. His job was to reach out over a little precipice to help the California girls out of their lift chairs. He would maintain his grasp until they were balanced upon the snow. And then he would release them, watch them descend the winter slope—how they laughed!—oblivious of his admiration, until they disappeared.

CHAPTER TWO

Late Victorians

St. Augustine writes from his cope of dust that we are restless hearts, for earth is not our true home. Human unhappiness is evidence of our immortality. Intuition tells us we are meant for some other city.

Elizabeth Taylor, quoted in a magazine article of twenty years ago, spoke of cerulean Richard Burton days on her yacht, days that were nevertheless undermined by the elemental private reflection: This must end.

■ ■ ■

On a Sunday in summer, ten years ago, I was walking home from the Latin mass at St. Patrick's, the old Irish parish downtown, when I saw thousands of people on Market Street. It was the Gay Freedom Day parade—not the first, but the first I ever saw. Private lives were becoming public. There were marching bands. There were floats. Banners blocked single lives thematically into a processional mass, not unlike the consortiums of the blessed in Renaissance paintings, each saint cherishing the apparatus of his martyrdom: GAY DENTISTS. BLACK AND WHITE LOVERS. GAYS FROM

BAKERSFIELD. LATINA LESBIANS. From the foot of Market Street they marched, east to west, following the mythic American path toward optimism.

I followed the parade to Civic Center Plaza, where flags of routine nations yielded sovereignty to a multitude. Pastel billows flowed over all.

Five years later, another parade. Politicians waved from white convertibles. "Dykes on Bikes" revved up, thumbs-upped. But now banners bore the acronyms of death. AIDS. ARC. Drums were muffled as passing, plum-spotted young men slid by on motorized cable cars.

Though I am alive now, I do not believe an old man's pessimism is necessarily truer than a young man's optimism simply because it comes after. There are things a young man knows that are true and are not yet in the old man's power to recollect. Spring has its sappy wisdom. Lonely teenagers still arrive in San Francisco aboard Greyhound buses. The city can still seem, by comparison with where they came from, paradise.

■ ■ ■

Four years ago on a Sunday in winter—a brilliant spring afternoon—I was jogging near Fort Point while overhead a young woman was, with difficulty, climbing over the railing of the Golden Gate Bridge. Holding down her skirt with one hand, with the other she waved to a startled spectator (the newspaper next day quoted a workman who was painting the bridge) before she stepped onto the sky.

To land like a spilled purse at my feet.

Serendipity has an eschatological tang here. Always has. Few American cities have had the experience, as we have had, of watching the civic body burn even as we stood, out of body, on a hillside, in a movie theater. Jeanette MacDonald's loony scatting of "San Francisco" has become our go-to-hell anthem. San Francisco has taken some heightened pleasure from the circus of final things. To Atlantis, to Pompeii, to the Pillar of Salt, we add the Golden Gate Bridge, not golden at all, but rust red. San Francisco toys with the tragic conclusion.

For most of its brief life, San Francisco has entertained an idea of itself as heaven on earth, whether as Gold Town or City Beautiful or the Haight-Ashbury.

San Francisco can support both comic and tragic conclusions because the city is geographically *in extremis*, a metaphor for the farthest-flung possibility, a metaphor for the end of the line. Land's end.

To speak of San Francisco as land's end is to read the map from one direction only—as Europeans would read it or as the East Coast has always read. In my lifetime San Francisco has become an Asian city. To speak, therefore, of San Francisco as land's end is to betray parochialism. My parents came here from Mexico. They saw San Francisco as the North. The West was not west for them. They did not share the Eastern traveler's sense of running before the past—the darkening time zone, the lowering curtain.

I cannot claim for myself the memory of a skyline such as the one César saw. César came to San Francisco in middle age; César came here as to some final place. He was born in South America; he had grown up in Paris; he had been everywhere, done everything; he assumed the world. Yet César was not condescending toward San Francisco, not at all. Here César saw revolution, and he embraced it.

Whereas I live here because I was born here. I grew up ninety miles away, in Sacramento. San Francisco was the nearest, the easiest, the inevitable city, since I needed a city. And yet I live here surrounded by people for whom San Francisco is the end of quest.

Late Victorians

I have never looked for utopia on a map. Of course I believe in human advancement. I believe in medicine, in astrophysics, in washing machines. But my compass takes its cardinal point from tragedy. If I respond to the metaphor of spring, I nevertheless learned, years ago, from my Mexican father, from my Irish nuns, to count on winter. The point of Eden for me, for us, is not approach but expulsion.

After I met César in 1984, our friendly debate concerning the halcyon properties of San Francisco ranged from restaurant to restaurant. I spoke of limits. César boasted of freedoms.

It was César's conceit to add to the gates of Jerusalem, to add to the soccer fields of Tijuana, one other dreamscape hoped for the world over. It was the view from a hill, through a mesh of tram wires, of an urban neighborhood in a valley. The vision took its name from the protruding wedge of a theater marquee. Here César raised his glass without discretion: To the Castro.

■ ■ ■

There were times, dear César, when you tried to switch sides, if only to scorn American optimism, which, I remind you, had already become your own. At the high school where César taught, teachers and parents had organized a campaign to keep kids from driving themselves to the junior prom, in an attempt to forestall liquor and death. Such a scheme momentarily reawakened César's Latin skepticism.

Didn't the Americans know? (His tone exaggerated incredulity.) Teenagers will crash into lampposts on their way home from proms, and there is nothing to be done about it. You cannot forbid tragedy.

■ ■ ■

By California standards I live in an old house. But not haunted. There are too many tall windows, there is too much salty light, especially in winter, though the windows rattle, rattle in summer when the fog flies overhead, and the house creaks and prowls at night. I feel myself immune to any confidence it seeks to tell.

To grow up homosexual is to live with secrets and within secrets. In no other place are those secrets more closely guarded than within the family home. The grammar of the gay city borrows metaphors from the nineteenth-century house. "Coming out of the closet" is predicated upon family laundry, dirty linen, skeletons.

I live in a tall Victorian house that has been converted to four apartments; four single men.

Neighborhood streets are named to honor nineteenth-century men of action, men of distant fame. Clay. Jackson. Scott. Pierce. Many Victorians in the neighborhood date from before the 1906 earthquake and fire.

Architectural historians credit the gay movement of the 1970s with the urban restoration of San Francisco. Twenty years ago this was a borderline neighborhood. This room, like all the rooms of the house, was painted headache green, apple green, boardinghouse green. In the 1970s, homosexuals moved into black and working-class parts of the city, where they were perceived as pioneers or as block-busters, depending.

Two decades ago, some of the least expensive sections of San Francisco were wooden Victorian sections. It was thus a coincidence of the market that gay men found themselves living within the architectural metaphor for family. No other architecture in the American imagination is more evocative of family than the Victorian house. In those same years—the 1970s—and within those same Victorian houses, homosexuals were living rebellious lives to challenge the foundations of domesticity.

Was "queer-bashing" as much a manifestation of homophobia as a reaction against gentrification? One heard the complaint, often enough, that gay men were as promiscuous with their capital as otherwise, buying, fixing up, then selling and moving on. Two incomes, no children, described an unfair advantage. No sooner would flower boxes begin to appear than an anonymous reply was smeared on the sidewalk out front: KILL FAGGOTS.

The three- or four-story Victorian house, like the Victorian novel, was built to contain several generations and several classes under one roof, behind a single oaken door. What strikes me at odd moments is the confidence of Victorian architecture. Stairs, connecting one story with another, describe the confidence that bound generations together through time—confidence that the family would inherit the earth. The other day I noticed for the first time the vestige of a hinge on the topmost newel of the staircase. This must have been the hinge of a gate that kept infants upstairs so many years ago.

If Victorian houses assert a sturdy optimism by day, they are also associated in our imaginations with the Gothic—with shadows and cobwebby gimcrack, long corridors. The nineteenth century was remarkable for escalating optimism even as it excavated the backstairs, the descending architecture of nightmare—Freud's labor and Engels's.

I live on the second story, in rooms that have been rendered as empty as Yorick's skull—gutted, unrattled, in various ways unlocked—added skylights and new windows, new doors. The hallway remains the darkest part of the house.

This winter the hallway and lobby are being repainted to resemble an eighteenth-century French foyer. Of late we had walls and carpet of Sienese red; a baroque mirror hung in an alcove by the stairwell. Now we are to have enlightened austerity—black-and-white marble floors and faux masonry. A man comes in the afternoons to texture the walls with a sponge and a rag and to paint white mortar lines that create an illusion of permanence, of stone.

The renovation of Victorian San Francisco into dollhouses for libertines may have seemed, in the 1970s, an evasion of what the city was actually becoming. San Francisco's rows of storied houses proclaimed a multigenerational orthodoxy, all the while masking the city's unconventional soul. Elsewhere, meanwhile, domestic America was coming undone.

Suburban Los Angeles, the prototype for a new America, was characterized by a more apparently radical residential architecture. There was, for example, the work of Frank Gehry. In the 1970s, Gehry exploded the nuclear-family house, turning it inside out intellectually and in fact. Though, in a way, Gehry merely completed the logic of the postwar suburban tract house—with its one story, its sliding glass doors, Formica kitchen, two-car garage. The tract house exchanged privacy for mobility. Heterosexuals opted for the one-lifetime house, the freeway, the birth-control pill, minimalist fiction.

■   ■   ■

The age-old description of homosexuality is of a sin against nature. Moralistic society has always judged emotion literally. The homosexual was sinful because he had no kosher place to stick it. In attempting to drape the architecture of sodomy with art, homosexuals have lived for thousands of years against the expectations of nature. Barren as Shakers and, interestingly, as concerned with the small effect, homosexuals have made a covenant against nature. Homosexual survival lay in artifice, in plumage, in lampshades, sonnets, musical comedy, couture, syntax, religious ceremony, opera, lacquer, irony.

I once asked Byron, an interior decorator, if he had many homosexual clients. *"Mais non,"* said he, flexing his eyelids. "Queers don't need decorators. They were born knowing how. All this ASID stuff—tests and regulations—as if you can confer a homosexual diploma on a suburban housewife by granting her a discount card."

Late Victorians

A knack? The genius, we are beginning to fear in an age of AIDS, is irreplaceable—but does it exist? The question is whether the darling affinities are innate to homosexuality or whether they are compensatory. Why have so many homosexuals retired into the small effect, the ineffectual career, the stereotype, the card shop, the florist? *Be gentle with me?* Or do homosexuals know things others do not?

This way power lay. Once upon a time, the homosexual appropriated to himself a mystical province, that of taste. Taste, which is, after all, the insecurity of the middle class, became the homosexual's licentiate to challenge the rule of nature. (The fairy in his blood, he intimated.)

Deciding how best to stick it may be only an architectural problem or a question of physics or of engineering or of cabinetry. Nevertheless, society's condemnation forced the homosexual to find his redemption outside nature. *We'll put a little skirt here.* The impulse is not to create but to re-create, to sham, to convert, to sauce, to rouge, to fragrance, to prettify. No effect is too small or too ephemeral to be snatched away from nature, to be ushered toward the perfection of artificiality. *We'll bring out the highlights there.* The homosexual has marshaled the architecture of the straight world to the very gates of Versailles—that great Vatican of fairyland—beyond which power is tyrannized by leisure.

In San Francisco in the 1980s, the highest form of art became interior decoration. The glory hole was thus converted to an eighteenth-century foyer.

■　■　■

I live away from the street, in a back apartment, in two rooms. I use my bedroom as a visitor's room—the sleigh bed tricked up with shams into a sofa—whereas I rarely invite anyone into my library, the public room, where I write, the public gesture.

I read in my bedroom in the afternoon because the light is good

33

there, especially now, in winter, when the sun recedes from the earth.

There is a door in the south wall that leads to a balcony. The door was once a window. Inside the door, inside my bedroom, are twin green shutters. They are false shutters, of no function beyond wit. The shutters open into the room; they have the effect of turning my apartment inside out.

A few months ago I hired a man to paint the shutters green. I wanted the green shutters of Manet—you know the ones I mean—I wanted a weathered look, as of verdigris. For several days the painter labored, rubbing his paints into the wood and then wiping them off again. In this way he rehearsed for me decades of the ravages of weather. Yellow enough? Black?

The painter left one afternoon, saying he would return the next, leaving behind his tubes, his brushes, his sponges and rags. He never returned. Someone told me he has AIDS.

■　■　■

A black woman haunts California Street between the donut shop and the cheese store. She talks to herself—a debate, wandering, never advancing. Pedestrians who do not know her give her a wide berth. Somebody told me her story; I don't know whether it's true. Neighborhood merchants tolerate her presence as a vestige of dispirited humanity clinging to an otherwise dispiriting progress of "better" shops and restaurants.

Repainted façades extend now from Jackson Street south into what was once the heart of the "Mo"—black Fillmore Street. Today there are watercress sandwiches at three o'clock where recently there had been loudmouthed kids, hole-in-the-wall bars, pimps. Now there are tweeds and perambulators, matrons and nannies. Yuppies. And gays.

The gay-male revolution had greater influence on San Francisco in the 1970s than did the feminist revolution. Feminists, with whom I include lesbians—such was the inclusiveness of the feminist movement—were preoccupied with career, with escape from the house in order to create a sexually democratic city. Homosexual men sought to reclaim the house, the house that traditionally had been the reward for heterosexuality, with all its selfless tasks and burdens.

Leisure defined the gay-male revolution. The gay political movement began, by most accounts, in 1969 with the Stonewall riots in New York City, whereby gay men fought to defend the nonconformity of their leisure.

It was no coincidence that homosexuals migrated to San Francisco in the 1970s, for the city was famed as a playful place, more Catholic than Protestant in its eschatological intuition. In 1975, the state of California legalized consensual homosexuality, and about that same time Castro Street, southwest of downtown, began to eclipse Polk Street as the homosexual address in San Francisco. Polk Street was a string of bars. The Castro was an entire district. The Castro had Victorian houses and churches, bookstores and restaurants, gyms, dry cleaners, supermarkets, and an elected member of the Board of Supervisors. The Castro supported baths and bars, but there was nothing furtive about them. On Castro Street the light of day penetrated gay life through clear plate-glass windows. The light of day discovered a new confidence, a new politics. Also a new look—a noncosmopolitan, Burt Reynolds, butch-kid style: beer, ball games, Levi's, short hair, muscles.

Gay men who lived elsewhere in the city, in Pacific Heights or in the Richmond, often spoke with derision of "Castro Street clones," describing the look, or scorned what they called the ghettoization of homosexuality. To an older generation of homosexuals, the blatancy of Castro Street threatened the discreet compromise they had negotiated with a tolerant city.

As the Castro district thrived, Folsom Street, south of Market, also began to thrive, as if in contradistinction to the utopian Castro. Folsom Street was a warehouse district of puddled alleys and deserted corners. Folsom Street offered an assortment of leather bars—an evening's regress to the outlaw sexuality of the fifties, the forties, the nineteenth century, and so on—an eroticism of the dark, of the Reeperbahn, or of the guardsman's barracks.

The Castro district implied that sexuality was more crucial, that homosexuality was the central fact of identity. The Castro district, with its ice-cream parlors and hardware stores, was the revolutionary place.

Into which carloads of vacant-eyed teenagers from other districts or from middle-class suburbs would drive after dark, cruising the neighborhood for solitary victims.

The ultimate gay-basher was a city supervisor named Dan White, ex-cop, ex-boxer, ex-fireman, ex–altar boy. Dan White had grown up in the Castro district; he recognized the Castro revolution for what it was. Gays had achieved power over him. He murdered the mayor and he murdered the homosexual member of the Board of Supervisors.

■　■　■

Katherine, a sophisticate if ever there was one, nevertheless dismisses two men descending the aisle at the Opera House: "All so sleek and smooth-jowled and silver-haired—they don't seem real, poor darlings. It must be because they don't have children."

Lodged within Katherine's complaint is the perennial heterosexual annoyance with the homosexual's freedom from child-rearing, which does not so much place the homosexual beyond the pale as it relegates the homosexual outside "responsible" life.

It was the glamour of gay life, after all, as much as it was the feminist call to career, that encouraged heterosexuals in the 1970s to excuse themselves from nature, to swallow the birth-control pill. Who needs children? The gay bar became the paradigm for the singles bar. The gay couple became the paradigm for the selfish couple—all dressed up and everywhere to go. And there was the example of the gay house in illustrated life-style magazines. At the same time that suburban housewives were looking outside the home for fulfillment, gay men were reintroducing a new generation in the city—heterosexual men and women—to the complaisancies of the barren house.

Puritanical America dismissed gay camp followers as yuppies; the term means to suggest infantility. Yuppies were obsessive and awkward in their materialism. Whereas gays arranged a decorative life against a barren state, yuppies sought early returns —lives that were not to be all toil and spin. Yuppies, trained to careerism from the cradle, wavered in their pursuit of the Northern European ethic—indeed, we might now call it the pan-Pacific ethic—in favor of the Mediterranean, the Latin, the Catholic, the Castro, the Gay.

■ ■ ■

The international architectural idioms of Skidmore, Owings & Merrill, which defined the skyline of the 1970s, betrayed no awareness of any street-level debate concerning the primacy of play in San Francisco or of any human dramas resulting from urban redevelopment. The repellent office tower was a fortress raised against the sky, against the street, against the idea of a city. Offices were hives where money was made, and damn all.

In the 1970s, San Francisco divided between the interests of downtown and the pleasures of the neighborhoods. Neighborhoods asserted idiosyncrasy, human scale, light. San Francisco neighborhoods perceived downtown as working against their influence in determining what the city should be. Thus neighborhoods seceded from the idea of a city.

The gay movement rejected downtown as representing "straight" conformity. But was it possible that heterosexual Union Street was related to Castro Street? Was it possible that either was related to the Latino Mission district? Or to the Sino-Russian Richmond? San Francisco, though complimented worldwide for holding its center, was in fact without a vision of itself entire.

In the 1980s, in deference to the neighborhoods, City Hall would attempt a counterreformation of downtown, forbidding "Manhattanization." Shadows were legislated away from parks and playgrounds. Height restrictions were lowered beneath an existing skyline. Design, too, fell under the retrojurisdiction of the city planner's office. The Victorian house was presented to architects as a model of what the city wanted to uphold and to become. In heterosexual neighborhoods, one saw newly built Victorians. Downtown, postmodernist prescriptions for playfulness advised skyscrapers to wear party hats, buttons, comic mustaches. Philip Johnson yielded to the dollhouse impulse to perch angels atop one of his skyscrapers.

■ ■ ■

I can see downtown from my bedroom window. But days pass and I do not leave the foreground for the city. Most days my public impression of San Francisco is taken from Fillmore Street, from the anchorhold of the Lady of the Donut Shop.

She now often parades with her arms crossed over her breasts in an "X," the posture emblematic of prophecy. And yet gather her madness where she sits on the curb, chain-smoking, hugging her knees, while I disappear down Fillmore Street to make Xerox copies, to mail letters, to rent a video, to shop for dinner. I am soon pleased by the faint breeze from the city, the slight agitation of the homing crowds of singles, so intent upon the path of least resistance. I admire the prosperity of the corridor, the shop windows that beckon inward toward the perfected life-style, the little way of the City of St. Francis.

Turning down Pine Street, I am recalled by the prickly silhouette of St. Dominic's Church against the scrim of the western sky. I turn, instead, into the Pacific Heights Health Club.

In the 1970s, like a lot of men and women in this city, I joined a gym. My club, I've even caught myself calling it.

In the gay city of the 1970s, bodybuilding became an architectural preoccupation of the upper middle class. Bodybuilding is a parody of labor, a useless accumulation of the laborer's bulk and strength. No useful task is accomplished. And yet there is something businesslike about habitués, and the gym is filled with the punch-clock logic of the workplace. Machines clank and hum. Needles on gauges toll spent calories.

The gym is at once a closet of privacy and an exhibition gallery. All four walls are mirrored.

I study my body in the mirror. Physical revelation—nakedness—is no longer possible, cannot be desired, for the body is shrouded in meat and wears itself.

The intent is some merciless press of body against a standard, perfect mold. Bodies are "cut" or "pumped" or "buffed" as on an assembly line in Turin. A body becomes so many extrovert parts. Delts, pecs, lats, traps.

I harness myself in a Nautilus cage.

Lats become wings. For the gym is nothing if not the occasion for transcendence. From homosexual to autosexual . . .

I lift weights over my head, baring my teeth like an animal with the strain.

. . . to nonsexual. The effect of the overdeveloped body is the miniaturization of the sexual organs—of no function beyond wit.

Behold the ape become Blakean angel, revolving in an empyrean of mirrors.

■ ■ ■

The nineteenth-century mirror over the fireplace in my bedroom was purchased by a decorator from the estate of a man who died last year of AIDS. It is a top-heavy piece, confusing styles. Two ebony-painted columns support a frieze of painted glass above the mirror. The frieze depicts three bourgeois graces and a couple of free-range cherubs. The lake of the mirror has formed a cataract, and at its edges it is beginning to corrode.

Thus the mirror that now draws upon my room owns some bright curse, maybe—some memory not mine.

As I regard this mirror, I imagine St. Augustine's meditation slowly hardening into syllogism, passing down through centuries to confound us: evil is the absence of good.

We have become accustomed to figures disappearing from our landscape. Does this not lead us to interrogate the landscape?

With reason do we invest mirrors with the superstition of memory, for they, though glass, though liquid captured in a bay, are so often less fragile than we are. They—bright ovals, or rectangles, or rounds—bump down unscathed, unspilled through centuries, whereas we . . .

The man in the red baseball cap used to jog so religiously on Marina Green. By the time it occurs to me that I have not seen him for months, I realize he may be dead—not lapsed, not moved away. People come and go in the city, it's true. But in San Francisco death has become as routine an explanation for disappearance as Mayflower Van Lines.

AIDS, it has been discovered, is a plague of absence. Absence opened in the blood. Absence condensed into the fluid of passing emotion. Absence shot through opalescent tugs of semen to deflower the city.

Late Victorians

And then AIDS, it was discovered, is a nonmetaphorical disease, a disease like any other. Absence sprang from substance —a virus, a hairy bubble perched upon a needle, a platter of no intention served round: fever, blisters, a death sentence.

At first I heard only a few names—names connected, perhaps, with the right faces, perhaps not. People vaguely remembered, as through the cataract of this mirror, from dinner parties or from intermissions. A few articles in the press. The rumored celebrities. But within months the slow beating of the blood had found its bay.

One of San Francisco's gay newspapers, the *Bay Area Reporter*, began to accept advertisements from funeral parlors and casket makers, inserting them between the randy ads for leather bars and tanning salons. The *Reporter* invited homemade obituaries— lovers writing of lovers, friends remembering friends and the blessings of unexceptional life.

Peter. Carlos. Gary. Asel. Perry. Nikos.

Healthy snapshots accompany each annal. At the Russian River. By the Christmas tree. Lifting a beer. In uniform. A dinner jacket. A satin gown.

He was born in Puerto La Libertad, El Salvador.

He attended Apple Valley High School, where he was their first male cheerleader.

From El Paso. From Medford. From Germany. From Long Island.

I moved back to San Francisco in 1979. Oh, I had had some salad days elsewhere, but by 1979 I was a wintry man. I came here in order not to be distracted by the ambitions or, for that matter, the pleasures of others but to pursue my own ambition. Once here, though, I found the company of men who pursued an earthly paradise charming. Skepticism became my demeanor toward them—I was the dinner-party skeptic, a firm believer in Original Sin and in the limits of possibility.

Which charmed them.

He was a dancer.

He settled into the interior-design department of Gump's, where he worked until his illness.

He was a teacher.

César, for example.

César had an excellent mind. César could shave the rind from any assertion to expose its pulp and jelly. But César was otherwise ruled by pulp. César loved everything that ripened in time. Freshmen. Bordeaux. César could fashion liturgy from an artichoke. Yesterday it was not ready (cocking his head, rotating the artichoke in his hand over a pot of cold water). Tomorrow will be too late (Yorick's skull). Today it is perfect (as he lit the fire beneath the pot). We will eat it now.

If he's lucky, he's got a year, a doctor told me. If not, he's got two.

The phone rang. AIDS had tagged a friend. And then the phone rang again. And then the phone rang again. Michael had tested positive. Adrian, well, what he had assumed were shingles . . . Paul was back in the hospital. And César, dammit, César, even César, especially César.

That winter before his death, César traveled back to South America. On his return to San Francisco, he described to me how he had walked with his mother in her garden—his mother chafing her hands as if she were cold. But it was not cold, he said. They moved slowly. Her summer garden was prolonging itself this year, she said. The cicadas will not stop singing.

When he lay on his deathbed, César said everyone else he knew might get AIDS and die. He said I would be the only one spared—"spared" was supposed to have been chased with irony, I knew, but his voice was too weak to do the job. "You are too circumspect," he said then, wagging his finger upon the coverlet.

So I was going to live to see that the garden of earthly delights was, after all, only wallpaper—was that it, César? Hadn't I always said so? It was then I saw that the greater sin against heaven was my unwillingness to embrace life.

■ ■ ■

César said he found paradise at the baths. He said I didn't understand. He said if I had to ask about it, I might as well ask if a wife will spend eternity with Husband #1 or Husband #2.

The baths were places of good humor, that was Number One; there was nothing demeaning about them. From within cubicles men would nod at one another or not, but there was no sting of rejection, because one had at last entered a region of complete acceptance. César spoke of floating from body to body, open arms yielding to open arms in an angelic round.

The best night. That's easy, he said, the best night was spent in the pool with an antiques dealer—up to their necks in warm water—their two heads bobbing on an ocean of chlorine green, bawling Noël Coward songs.

But each went home alone?

Each satisfied, dear, César corrected. And all the way home San Francisco seemed to him balmed and merciful, he said. He felt weightlessness of being, the pavement under his step as light as air.

■ ■ ■

It was not as in some Victorian novel—the curtains drawn, the pillows plumped, the streets strewn with sawdust. It was not to be a matter of custards in covered dishes, steaming possets, *Try a little of this, my dear*. Or gathering up the issues of *Architectural*

Digest strewn about the bed. Closing the biography of Diana Cooper and marking its place. Or the unfolding of discretionary screens, morphine, parrots, pavilions.

César experienced agony.

Four of his high-school students sawed through a Vivaldi quartet in the corridor outside his hospital room, prolonging the hideous garden.

In the presence of his lover Gregory and friends, Scott passed from this life. . . .

He died peacefully at home in his lover Ron's arms.

Immediately after a friend led a prayer for him to be taken home and while his dear mother was reciting the 23rd Psalm, Bill peacefully took his last breath.

I stood aloof at César's memorial, the kind of party he would enjoy, everyone said. And so for a time César lay improperly buried, unconvincingly resurrected in the conditional: would enjoy. What else could they say? César had no religion beyond aesthetic bravery.

Sunlight remains. Traffic remains. Nocturnal chic attaches to some discovered restaurant. A new novel is reviewed in *The New York Times*. And the mirror rasps on its hook. The mirror is lifted down.

A priest friend, a good friend, who out of naïveté plays the cynic, tells me—this is on a bright, billowy day; we are standing outside—"It's not as sad as you may think. There is at least spectacle in the death of the young. Come to the funeral of an old lady sometime if you want to feel an empty church."

I will grant my priest friend this much: that it is easier, easier on me, to sit with gay men in hospitals than with the staring old. Young men talk as much as they are able.

But those who gather around the young man's bed do not see Chatterton. This doll is Death. I have seen people caressing it, staring Death down. I have seen people wipe its tears, wipe its ass; I have seen people kiss Death on his lips, where once there were lips.

Chris was inspired after his own diagnosis in July 1987 with the truth and reality of how such a terrible disease could bring out the love, warmth, and support of so many friends and family.

Sometimes no family came. If there was family, it was usually Mother. Mom. With her suitcase and with the torn flap of an envelope in her hand.

Brenda. Pat. Connie. Toni. Soledad.

Or parents came but then left without reconciliation, some preferring to say "cancer."

But others came. They walked Death's dog. They washed his dishes. They bought his groceries. They massaged his poor back. They changed his bandages. They emptied his bedpan.

Men who sought the aesthetic ordering of existence were recalled to nature. Men who aspired to the mock-angelic settled for the shirt of hair. The gay community of San Francisco, having found freedom, consented to necessity—to all that the proud world had for so long held up to them, withheld from them, as "real humanity."

And if gays took care of their own, they were not alone. AIDS was a disease of the entire city. Nor were Charity and Mercy only male, only gay. Others came. There were nurses and nuns and the couple from next door, co-workers, strangers, teenagers, corporations, pensioners. A community was forming over the city.

Cary and Rick's friends and family wish to thank the many people who provided both small and great kindnesses.

He was attended to and lovingly cared for by the staff at Coming Home Hospice.

And the saints of this city have names listed in the phone book, names I heard called through a microphone one cold Sunday in

Advent as I sat in Most Holy Redeemer Church. It might have been any of the churches or community centers in the Castro district, but it happened at Most Holy Redeemer at a time in the history of the world when the Roman Catholic Church pronounced the homosexual a sinner.

A woman at the microphone called upon volunteers from the AIDS Support Group to come forward. Throughout the church, people stood up, young men and women, and middle-aged and old, straight, gay, and all of them shy at being called. Yet they came forward and assembled in the sanctuary, facing the congregation, grinning self-consciously at one another, their hands hidden behind them.

I am preoccupied by the fussing of a man sitting in the pew directly in front of me—in his seventies, frail, his iodine-colored hair combed forward and pasted upon his forehead. Fingers of porcelain clutch the pearly beads of what must have been his mother's rosary. He is not the sort of man any gay man would have chosen to become in the 1970s. He is probably not what he himself expected to become. Something of the old dear about him, wizened butterfly, powdered old pouf. Certainly he is what I fear becoming. And then he rises, this old monkey, with the most beatific dignity, in answer to the microphone, and he strides into the sanctuary to take his place in the company of the Blessed.

So this is it—this, what looks like a Christmas party in an insurance office, and not as in Renaissance paintings, and not as we had always thought, not some flower-strewn, some sequined curtain call of greasepainted heroes gesturing to the stalls. A lady with a plastic candy cane pinned to her lapel. A Castro clone with a red bandana exploding from his hip pocket. A perfume-counter lady with an Hermès scarf mantled upon her shoulder. A black man in a checkered sports coat. The pink-haired punkess with a jewel in her nose. Here, too, is the gay couple in middle age; interchangeable plaid shirts and corduroy pants. Blood and shit and Mr. Happy Face. These know the weight of bodies.

Bill died.

. . . Passed on to heaven.

. . . Turning over in his bed one night and then gone.

These learned to love what is corruptible, while I, barren skeptic, reader of St. Augustine, curator of the earthly paradise, inheritor of the empty mirror, I shift my tailbone upon the cold, hard pew.

CHAPTER THREE

Mexico's Children

When I was a boy it was still possible for Mexican farmworkers in California to commute between the past and the future.

The past returned every October. The white sky clarified to blue and fog opened white fissures in the landscape.

After the tomatoes and the melons and the grapes had been picked, it was time for Mexicans to load up their cars and head back into Mexico for the winter.

The schoolteacher said aloud to my mother what a shame it was the Mexicans did that—took their children out of school.

Like wandering Jews, Mexicans had no true home but the tabernacle of memory.

The schoolteacher was scandalized by what she took as the Mexicans' disregard of their children's future. The children failed their tests. They made no friends. What did it matter? Come November, they would be gone to some bright world that smelled like the cafeteria on Thursdays—Bean Days. Next spring they would be enrolled in some other school, in some other Valley town.

The schoolroom myth of America described an ocean—immigrants leaving behind several time zones and all the names for things.

Mexican-American memory described proximity. There are large Mexican-American populations in Seattle and Chicago and Kansas City, but the majority of Mexican Americans live, where most have always lived, in the Southwestern United States, one or two hours from Mexico, which is within the possibility of recourse to Mexico or within the sound of her voice.

My father knew men in Sacramento who had walked up from Mexico.

There is confluence of earth. The cut of the land or its fold, the bleaching sky, the swath of the wind, the length of shadows—all these suggested Mexico. Mitigated was the sense of dislocation otherwise familiar to immigrant experience.

By November the fog would thicken, the roads would be dangerous. Better to be off by late October. Families in old trucks and cars headed south down two-lane highways, past browning fields. Rolls of toilet paper streaming from rolled-down windows. After submitting themselves to the vegetable cycle of California for a season, these Mexicans were free. They were Mexicans! And what better thing to be?

HAIIII-EEE. HAI. HAI. HAI.

There is confluence of history.

Cities, rivers, mountains retain Spanish names. California was once Mexico.

The fog closes in, condenses, and drips day and night from the bare limbs of trees. And my mother looks out the kitchen window and cannot see the neighbor's house.

Amnesia fixes the American regard of the past. I remember a graduate student at Columbia University during the Vietnam years; she might have been an ingenue out of Henry James. "After

Vietnam, I'll never again believe that America is the good and pure country I once thought it to be," the young woman said.

Whereas Mexican Americans have paid a price for the clarity of their past.

Consider my father: when he decided to apply for American citizenship, my father told no one, none of his friends, those men with whom he had come to this country looking for work. American citizenship would have seemed a betrayal of Mexico, a sin against memory. One afternoon, like a man with something to hide, my father slipped away. He went downtown to the Federal Building in Sacramento and disappeared into America.

Now memory takes her revenge on the son.

■ ■ ■

VETE PERO NO ME OLVIDES.

Go, but do not forget me, someone has written on the side of a building near the border in Tijuana.

Mexicans may know their souls are imperiled in America but they do not recognize the risk by its proper name.

Two Mexican teenagers say they are going to *los Estados Unidos* for a job. Nothing more.

For three or four generations now, Mexican villages have lived under the rumor of America, a rumor vaguer than paradise. America exists in thousands of maternal prayers and in thousands of pubescent dreams. Everyone knows someone who has been. Everyone knows someone who never came back.

What do you expect to find?

The answer is always an explanation for the journey: "I want money enough to be able to return to live with my family in Mexico."

Proofs of America's existence abound in Mexican villages— stereo equipment, for example, or broken-down cars—but these are things Americans picked up or put down, not America.

50

Mexico's Children

Mexicans know very little of the United States, though they have seen America, the TV show, and America, the movie. Mexico's pre-eminent poet, Octavio Paz, writes of the United States as an idea of no characteristic mansion or spice. Paz has traveled and taught in America, but his writings relegate America to ineluctability—a jut of optimism, an aerodynamic law.

To enter America, which is invisible, Mexicans must become invisible. Tonight, a summer night, five hundred Mexicans will become invisible at 8:34 P.M. While they wait, they do not discuss Tom Paine or Thomas Jefferson or the Bill of Rights. Someone has an uncle in Los Angeles who knows a peach farmer near Tracy who always hires this time of year.

Compared with pulpy Mexico, grave Mexico, sandstone Mexico, which takes the impression of time, the United States and its promise of the future must seem always hypothetical—occasion more than place.

I once had occasion to ask a middle-class Mexican what he admires about the United States (a provocative question because, according to Mexican history and proverb, there is nothing about the United States to admire). He found only one disembodied word: "organization." When I pressed the man to anthropomorphize further he said, "Deliveries get made, phones are answered, brakes are repaired" (indirect constructions all, as if by the consent of unseen hands).

Coming from Mexico, a country that is so thoroughly *there*, where things are not necessarily different from when your father was your age, Mexicans are unable to puncture the abstraction. For Mexicans, even death is less abstract than America.

Mexican teenagers waiting along the levee in Tijuana are bound to be fooled by the United States because they do not yet realize the future will be as binding as the past. The American job will introduce the Mexican to an industry, an optimism, a solitude nowhere described in Mexico's theology.

How can two Mexican teenagers know this, clutching the paper bags their mamas packed for them this morning? The past is already the future, for the bags contain only a change of underwear. These two may have seen *Dallas* on TV and they may think they are privy to the logic and locution of America. But that is not the same thing as having twenty American dollars in their own pockets.

■   ■   ■

Mexico, mad mother. She still does not know what to make of our leaving. For most of this century Mexico has seen her children flee the house of memory. During the Revolution 10 percent of the population picked up and moved to the United States; in the decades following the Revolution, Mexico has watched many more of her children cast their lots with the future; head north for work, for wages; north for life. Bad enough that so many left, worse that so many left her for the gringo.

America wanted cheap labor. American contractors reached down into Mexico for men to build America. Sons followed fathers north. It became a rite of passage for the poor Mexican male.

I will send for you or I will come home rich.

I would see them downtown on Sundays—men my age drunk in Plaza Park. I was still a boy at sixteen, but I was an American. At sixteen, I wrote a gossip column, "The Watchful Eye," for my school paper.

Or they would come into town on Monday nights for the wrestling matches or on Tuesday nights for boxing. They worked on ranches over in Yolo County. They were men with time on their hands. They were men without women. They were Mexicans without Mexico.

Mexico's Children

On Saturdays, Mexican men flooded the Western Union office, where they sent money—money turned into humming wire and then turned back into money—all the way down into Mexico. America was a monastery. America was a vow of poverty. They kept themselves poor for Mexico.

Fidel, the janitor at church, lived over the garage at the rectory. Fidel spoke Spanish and was Mexican. He had a wife down there, people said; some said he had grown children. But too many years had passed and he didn't go back. Fidel had to do for himself. Fidel had a clean piece of linoleum on the floor; he had an iron bed; he had a table and a chair; he had a frying pan and a knife and a fork and a spoon. Everything else Fidel sent back to Mexico. Sometimes, on summer nights, I would see his head through the bars of the little window over the garage of the rectory.

My parents left Mexico in the twenties: she as a girl with her family; he as a young man, alone. To tell different stories. Two Mexicos. At some celebration—we went to so many when I was a boy—a man in the crowd filled his lungs with American air to crow over all, ¡VIVA MEXICO! Everyone cheered. My parents cheered. The band played louder. Why VIVA MEXICO? The country that had betrayed them? The country that had forced them to live elsewhere?

I remember standing in the doorway of my parents' empty bedroom.

Mexico was memory—not mine. Mexico was mysteriously both he and she, like this, like my parents' bed. And over my parents' bed floated the Virgin of Guadalupe in a dimestore frame. In its most potent guise, Mexico was a mother like this queen. Her lips curved like a little boat. *Tú. Tú.* The suspirate vowel. *Tú.* The ruby pendant. The lemon tree. The song of the dove. Breathed through the nose, perched on the lips.

Two voices, two pronouns were given me as a child, like good and bad angels, like sweet and sour milks, like rank and clement weathers; one yielding, one austere.

In the sixteenth century, Spain bequeathed to Mexico two forms of address, two versions of "you": In Mexico there is *tú* and there is *usted*.

In Sacramento, California, everything outside our house was English, was "you"—hey you. My dog was you. My parents were you. The nuns were you. My best friend, my worst enemy was you. God was You.

Whereas the architecture of Mexico is the hardened shell of a Spanish distinction.

Treeless, open plazas abate at walls; walls yield to refreshment, to interior courtyards, to shuttered afternoons.

At the heart there is *tú*—the intimate voice—the familiar room in a world full of rooms. *Tú* is the condition, not so much of knowing, as of being known; of being recognized. *Tú* belongs within the family. *Tú* is spoken to children and dogs, to priests; among lovers and drunken friends; to servants; to statues; to the high court of heaven; to God Himself.

The shaded arcade yields once more to the plaza, to traffic and the light of day. *Usted,* the formal, the bloodless, the ornamental you, is spoken to the eyes of strangers. By servants to masters. *Usted* shows deference to propriety, to authority, to history. *Usted* is open to interpretation; therefore it is subject to corruption, a province of politicians. *Usted* is the language outside Eden.

■ ■ ■

In Mexico, one is most oneself in private. The very existence of *tú* must undermine the realm of *usted*. In America, one is most oneself in public.

In order to show you America I would have to take you out. I would take you to the restaurant—OPEN 24 HOURS—alongside a freeway, any freeway in the U.S.A. The waitress is a blond or a redhead—not the same color as at her last job. She is divorced. Her eyebrows are jet-black migraines painted on, or relaxed, clownish domes of cinnamon brown. Morning and the bloom of youth are painted on her cheeks. She is at once antimaternal—the kind of woman you're not supposed to know—and supramaternal, the nurturer of lost boys.

She is the priestess of the short order, curator of the apple pie. She administers all the consolation of America. She has no illusions. She knows the score; she hands you the Bill of Rights printed on plastic, decorated with an heraldic tumble of French fries and drumsticks and steam.

Your table may yet be littered with bitten toast and spilled coffee and a dollar tip. Now you will see the greatness of America. As one complete gesture, the waitress pockets the tip, stacks dishes along one strong forearm, produces a damp rag soaked in lethe water, which she then passes over the Formica.

There! With that one swipe of the rag, the past has been obliterated. The Formica gleams like new. You can order anything you want.

If I were to show you Mexico, I would take you home; with the greatest reluctance I would take you home, where family snapshots crowd upon the mantel. For the Mexican, the past is firmly held from within. While outside, a few miles away in the American city, there is only loosening, unraveling; generations living apart. Old ladies living out their lives in fiercely flowered housedresses. Their sons are divorced; wear shorts, ride bikes; are not men, really; not really. Their granddaughters are not fresh, are not lovely or keen, are not even nice.

Seek the Mexican in the embrace of the family, where there is much noise. The family stands as a consolation, because in the certainty of generation there is protection against an uncertain

55

future. At the center of this gravity the child is enshrined. He is not rock-a-bye baby at the very top of the family tree, as it is with American families. The child does not represent distance from the past, but reflux. She is not expected to fly away, to find herself. He is not expected to live his own life.

I will send for you or I will come home rich.

The culture of *tú* is guarded by the son, desired by the son, enforced by the son. Femininity is defined by the son as motherhood. Only a culture so cruel to the wife could sustain such a sentimental regard for *mamacita*. By contrast, much license is appropriated by the Mexican male. If the brother is taught to hover—he is guarding his sister's virginity—the adolescent male is otherwise, elsewhere, schooled in seduction. For the male as for the female, sexuality is expressed as parenthood. The male, by definition, is father. The husband is always a son.

It is not coincidental that American feminists have borrowed the Spanish word *macho* to name their American antithesis. But in English, the macho is publicly playful, boorish, counterdomestic. American macho is drag—the false type for the male—as Mae West is the false type for the female.

Machismo in Mexican Spanish is more akin to the Latin *gravitas*. The male is serious. The male provides. The Mexican male never abandons those who depend upon him. The male remembers.

Mexican *machismo*, like Mexican politics, needs its mise-en-scène. In fair Verona, in doublet and hose, it might yet play. The male code derives less from efficacy than from valor. *Machismo* is less an assertion of power or potency than it is a rite of chivalry.

The *macho* is not urbane Gilbert Roland or the good guy Lee Trevino; he is more like Bobby Chacon, the slight, leathery, middle-aged boxer, going twelve rounds the night after his wife commits suicide. The *macho* holds his own ground. There is sobriety in the male, and silence, too—a severe limit on emotional range. The male isn't weak. The male wins a Purple Heart or he turns wife beater. The male doesn't cry.

Men sing in Mexico. In song, the male can admit longing, pain, desire, weakness.

HAIII-EEEE.

A cry like a comet rises over the song. A cry like mock-weeping tickles the refrain of Mexican love songs. The cry is meant to encourage the balladeer—it is the raw edge of his sentiment. HAI-II-EEE. It is the man's sound. A ticklish arching of semen, a node wrung up a guitar string, until it bursts in a descending cascade of mockery. HAI. HAI. HAI. The cry of the jackal under the moon, the whistle of the phallus, the maniacal song of the skull.

So it may well be Mama who first realizes the liberation of the American "you," the American pan-*usted*, the excalibur "I" which will deliver her from the Islamic cloister of Mexico. (*Tú.*)

■ ■ ■

A true mother, Mexico would not distinguish among her children. Her protective arm extended not only to the Mexican nationals working in the United States, but to the larger number of Mexican Americans as well. Mexico was not interested in passports; Mexico was interested in blood. No matter how far away you moved, you were still related to her.

In 1943, American sailors in Los Angeles ventured into an evil vein of boredom. They crashed the east side of town, where they beat up barrio teenagers dressed in the punk costume of their day. "The Zoot Suit Riots" lasted several nights. City officials went to bed early, and the Los Angeles press encouraged what it termed high-spirited sailors. It required the diplomatic protest of the Mexican ambassador and the consequent intervention of the U.S. secretary of state to end the disturbances.

Mexico sent cables of protest to Washington whenever she heard of the mistreatment of Mexican nationals. In a city as small as Sacramento in the 1950s, there was a Mexican consulate—a small white building downtown, in all ways like an insurance office, except for the seal of Mexico over the door. For decades, at offices like this one, Mexicans would find a place of defense in the U.S.A.

In 1959, Octavio Paz, Mexico's sultan son, her clever one— philosopher, poet, statesman—published *The Labyrinth of Solitude*, his reflections on Mexico. Within his labyrinth, Paz places as well the Mexican American. He writes of the *pachuco*, the teenage gang member, and, by implication, of the Mexican American: "The *pachuco* does not want to become a Mexican again; at the same time he does not want to blend into the life of North America. His whole being is sheer negative impulse, a tangle of contradictions, an enigma."

This was Mother Mexico talking, her good son; this was Mexico's metropolitan version of Mexican Americans. Mexico had lost language, lost gods, lost ground. Mexico recognized historical confusion in us. We were Mexico's Mexicans.

When we return to Mexico as *turistas*, with our little wads of greenbacks, our credit cards, our Japanese cameras, our Bermuda shorts, our pauses for directions and our pointing fingers, Mexico condescends to take our order (our order in halting Spanish), *claro señor*. But the table is not cleared; the table will never be cleared. Mexico prefers to reply in English, as a way of saying:
¡Pocho!

The Mexican American who forgets his true mother is a *pocho*, a person of no address, a child of no proper idiom.

But blood is blood, or perhaps, in this case, language is blood. Mexico worried. Mexico had seen her children lured by the gringo's offer of work. During the Great Depression, as the gringo's eyes slowly drained of sugar, thousands of Mexicans in the United States were rounded up and deported.

In 1938, my mother's brother returned to Mexico with only a curse for the United States of America. He had worked at construction sites throughout California and he was paid less than he had contracted for. At his stupefaction—the money in his hand—the contractor laughed.

What's the matter, babe, can't you Mesicans count?

And who took him back, shrieks Mexico, thumping her breast. Who?

No wonder that Mexico would not entertain the idea of a "Mexican American" except as a fiction, a bad joke of history. And most Mexican Americans lived in barrios, apart from gringos; many retained Spanish, as if in homage to her. We were still her children.

As long as we didn't marry.

■ ■ ■

His coming of age.

From his bed he watches Mama moving back and forth under the light. Outside, the bells of the church fly through the dark. Mama crosses herself. He pushes back the plastic curtain until his nostril catches air. He turns toward Mama. He studies her back —it is like a loaf of bread—as she bends over the things she is wrapping for him to take.

Today he becomes a man. His father has sent for him. His father has sent an address in the American city. That's what it means. His father is in the city with his uncle. He remembers his uncle remembering snow with his beer.

The boy dresses in the shadows. Then he moves toward the table, the circle of light. He sits down. He forces himself to eat. Mama stands over him to make the sign of the cross with her thumb on his forehead. He smiles for her. She puts a bag of food in his hands. She says she has told La Virgen to watch over him.

Yes, and he leaves quickly. Outside it is gray. He hears a little breeze. Or is it the rustle of old black Dueña, the dog—yes, it is she—taking her shortcuts through the weeds, crazy Dueña, her pads through the dust, following him. He passes the houses of the village; each window has a proper name. He passes Muñoz, the store. Old Rosa, the bar. The lighted window of the clinic where the pale medical student from Monterrey lives alone and reads his book full of sores late into the night.

The boy has just passed beyond the cemetery. His guardian breeze has died. The sky has begun to lighten. He turns and throws a rock back at La Dueña—it might be his heart that he throws. But no need. She will not go past the cemetery, not even for him. She will turn in circles like a loca and bite herself, Old Dueña, saying her rosary.

The dust takes on gravel, the path becomes a rutted road which leads to the highway. He walks north. The sky has turned white. Insects click in the fields. In time, there will be a bus.

■ ■ ■

The endurance of Mexico may be attributed to the realm of *tú*, wherein the family, the village, is held in immutable suspension; whereby the city—the government—is held in contempt.

Mexicans will remember this century as the century of loss. The land of Mexico will not sustain Mexicans. For generations, from Mexico City, came promises of land reform. *The land will be yours.*

What more seductive promise could there be to a nation haunted by the memory of dispossession?

The city broke most of its promises.

Mexico's Children

The city represents posture and hypocrisy to the average Mexican. The average Mexican imagination will weigh the city against the village and come up short. But the city represents the only possibility for survival. In the last half of this century, Mexicans have abandoned the village. And there is no turning back. After generations of ancestors asleep beneath the earth and awake above the sky, after roosters and priests and sleeping dogs, there is only the city.

The Goddess of Liberty—that stony schoolmarm—may well ask Mexicans why they are so resistant to change, to the interesting freedoms she offers. Mexicans are notorious in the United States for their skepticism regarding public life. Mexicans don't vote. Mexicans drop out of school.

Mexicans live in superstitious fear of the American diaspora. Mexican Americans are in awe of education, of getting too much schooling, of changing too much, of moving too far from home.

Well, now. Never to be outdone, Mother Mexico has got herself up in goddess cloth. She carries a torch, too, and it is the torch of memory. She is searching for her children.

A false mother, Mexico cares less for her children than for her pride. The exodus of so many Mexicans for the U.S. is not evidence of Mexico's failure; it is evidence, rather, of the emigrant's failure. After all, those who left were of the peasant, the lower classes—those who could not make it in Mexico.

The government of hurt pride is not above political drag. The government of Mexico impersonates the intimate genius of matriarchy in order to justify a political stranglehold.

In its male, in its public, in its city aspect, Mexico is an archtransvestite, a tragic buffoon. Dogs bark and babies cry when Mother Mexico walks abroad in the light of day. The policeman, the Marxist mayor—Mother Mexico doesn't even bother to shave her mustachios. Swords and rifles and spurs and bags of money

61

chink and clatter beneath her skirts. A chain of martyred priests dangles from her waist, for she is an austere, pious lady. Ay, how much—clutching her jangling bosoms; spilling cigars—how much she has suffered!

REMEMBER. THE STRENGTH OF MEXICO IS THE FAMILY. (A government billboard.)

■ ■ ■

In his glass apartment overlooking the Polanco district of Mexico City, the journalist says he does not mind in the least that I call myself an American. "But when I hear Mexicans in the United States talk about George Washington as the father of their country," he exhales a florid ellipsis of cigarette smoke.

■ ■ ■

America does not lend itself to sexual metaphor as easily as Mexico does. George Washington is the father of the country, we say. We speak of Founding Fathers. The legend ascribed to the Statue of Liberty is childlessness.

America is an immigrant country. Motherhood—parenthood—is less our point than adoption. If I had to assign gender to America, I would notice the consensus of the rest of the world. When America is burned in effigy, a male is burned. Americans themselves speak of Uncle Sam. Uncle Sam is the personification of conscription.

During World War II, hundreds of thousands of Mexican Americans were drafted to fight in Europe and in Asia. And they went, submitting themselves to a commonweal. Not a very Mexican thing to do, for Mexico had taught us always that we lived apart from history in the realm of *tú*.

It was Uncle Sam who shaved the sideburns from that generation of Mexican Americans. Like the Goddess of Liberty, Uncle Sam has no children of his own. In a way, Sam represents necessary evil to the American imagination. He steals children to make men of them, mocks all reticence, all modesty, all memory. Uncle Sam is a hectoring Yankee, a skinflint uncle, gaunt, uncouth, unloved. He is the American Savonarola—hater of moonshine, destroyer of stills, burner of cocaine. Free enterprise is curiously an evasion of Uncle Sam, as is sentimentality. Sam has no patience with mamas' boys. That includes Mama Mexico, ma'am.

You betray Uncle Sam by favoring private over public life, by seeking to exempt yourself: by cheating on your income taxes, by avoiding jury duty, by trying to keep your boy on the farm. These are legal offenses.

Betrayal of Mother Mexico, on the other hand, is a sin against the natural law, a failure of memory.

When the war was over, Mexican Americans returned home to a GI Bill and with the expectation of an improved future. By the 1950s, Mexican Americans throughout the Southwest were busy becoming middle-class. I would see them around Sacramento: a Mexican-American dentist; a shoe salesman at Weinstock's; the couple that ran the tiny Mexican food store that became, before I graduated from high school, a block-long electrified MEXICA-TESSEN. These were not "role models," exactly; they were people like my parents, making their way in America.

■ ■ ■

When I was in grammar school, they used to hit us for speaking Spanish.

THEY.

Mexican Americans forfeit the public experience of America because we fear it. And for decades in the American Southwest, public life was withheld from us. America lay north of *usted*, beyond even formal direct address. America was the realm of *los norteamericanos*—They. We didn't have an adequate name for you. In private, you were the gringo. The ethnic albino. The goyim. The ghost. You were not us. In public we also said

"Anglo"—an arcane usage of the nineteenth century—you-who-speak-English. If we withdrew from directly addressing you, you became *ellos*—They—as in: They kept us on the other side of town. They owned the land. They owned the banks. They ran the towns—they and their wives in their summer-print dresses. They kept wages low. They made us sit upstairs in the movie houses. Or downstairs.

Thus spoken memory becomes a kind of shorthand for some older, other outrage, the nineteenth-century affront. The land stolen. The Mexican scorned on land he had named. Spic. Greaser. Spanish, the great metropolitan language, reduced to a foreign tongue, a language of the outskirts, the language of the gibbering poor, thus gibberish; English, the triumphal, crushing metaphor.

I know Mexican Americans who have lived in this country for forty or fifty years and have never applied for citizenship or gathered more than a Montgomery Ward sense of English. Their refusal, lodged between *How much* and *Okay,* is not a linguistic dilemma primarily.

On the other hand, when we call ourselves Mexican Americans, Mexico is on the phone, long-distance: *So typical of the gringo's arrogance to appropriate the name of a hemisphere to himself—yes? But why should you repeat the folly?*

Mexico always can find a myth to account for us: Mexicans who go north are like the Chichimeca—a barbarous tribe antithetical to Mexico. But in the United States, Mexican Americans did not exist in the national imagination until the 1960s—years when the black civil-rights movement prompted Americans to acknowledge "invisible minorities" in their midst. Then it was determined statistically that Mexican Americans constituted a disadvantaged society, living in worse conditions than most other

Americans, having less education, facing bleaker sidewalks or Safeways.

Bueno. (Again Mother Mexico is on the phone.) *What kind of word is that—"minority"? Was the Mexican American*—she fries the term on the skillet of her tongue—*was the Mexican American content to say that his association with Mexico left him culturally disadvantaged?*

The sixties were years of romance for the American middle class. Americans competed with one another to play the role of society's victim. It was an age of T-shirts.

In those years, the national habit of Americans was to seek from the comparison with blacks a kind of analogy. Mexican-American political activists, especially student activists, insisted on a rough similarity between the two societies—black, Chicano—ignoring any complex factor of history or race that might disqualify the equation.

Black Americans had suffered relentless segregation and mistreatment, but blacks had been implicated in the public life of this country from the beginning. Oceans separated the black slave from any possibility of rescue or restoration. From the symbiosis of oppressor and the oppressed, blacks took a hard realism. They acquired the language of the white man, though they inflected it with refusal. And because racism fell upon all blacks, regardless of class, a bond developed between the poor and the bourgeoisie, thence the possibility of a leadership class able to speak for the entire group.

Mexican Americans of the generation of the sixties had no myth of themselves as Americans. So that when Mexican Americans won national notoriety, we could only refer the public gaze to the past. We are people of the land, we told ourselves. Middle-class college students took to wearing farmer-in-the-dell overalls and they took, as well, a rural slang to name themselves: Chicanos.

Chicanismo blended nostalgia with grievance to reinvent the mythic northern kingdom of Atzlán as corresponding to the Southwestern American desert. Just as Mexico would only celebrate her Indian half, Chicanos determined to portray themselves as Indians in America, as indigenous people, thus casting the United States in the role of Spain.

Chicanos used the language of colonial Spain to declare to America that they would never give up their culture. And they said, in Spanish, that Spaniards had been oppressors of their people.

Left to ourselves in a Protestant land, Mexican Americans shored up our grievances, making of them altars to the past. *May my tongue cleave to my palate if I should forget thee. (Tú.)*

Ah, Mother, can you not realize how Mexican we have become? But she hates us, she hates us.

Chicanismo offended Mexico. It was one thing for Mexico to play the victim among her children, but Mexico did not like it that Chicanos were playing the same role for the gringos.

By claiming too many exemptions, Chicanos also offended Americans. Chicanos seemed to violate a civic agreement that generations of other immigrants had honored: *My* grandparents had to learn English. . . .

Chicanos wanted more and less than they actually said. On the one hand, Chicanos were intent upon bringing America (as a way of bringing history) to some Act of Contrition. On the other hand, Chicanos sought pride, a restoration of face in America. And America might provide the symbolic solution to a Mexican dilemma: if one could learn public English while yet retaining family Spanish, *usted* might be reunited with *tú*, the future might be reconciled with the past.

Mexicans are a people of sacraments and symbols. I think few

Chicanos ever expected Spanish to become a public language coequal with English. But by demanding Spanish in the two most symbolic places of American citizenship—the classroom and the voting booth—Chicanos were consoling themselves that they need not give up the past to participate in the American city. They were not less American for speaking Spanish; they were not less Mexican for succeeding in America.

America got bored with such altars—too Catholic for the likes of America. Protestant America is a literal culture.

SAY WHAT YOU WANT.

What was granted was a bureaucratic bilingualism—classrooms and voting booths—pragmatic concessions to a spiritual grievance.

I end up arguing about bilingualism with other Mexican Americans, middle-class like myself. As I am my father's son, I am skeptical, like Mexico; I play the heavy, which is to say I play America. We argue and argue, but not about pedagogy. We argue about desire's reach; we exchange a few platitudes (being richer for having two languages; being able to go home again). In the end, the argument reduces to somebody's childhood memory.

When I was in school, they used to hit us for speaking Spanish.

My father says the trouble with the bilingual voting ballot is that one ends up voting for the translator.

■ ■ ■

In the late 1960s, when César Chávez made the cover of *Time* as the most famous Mexican American anyone could name, he was already irrelevant to Mexican-American lives insofar as 90 percent of us lived in cities and we were more apt to work in construction than as farmworkers. My mother, who worked downtown, and my father, who worked downtown, nevertheless sent money to César Chávez, because the hardness of his struggle on the land reminded them of the hardness of their Mexican past.

I remember the farmworkers' "Lenten Pilgrimage" through California's Central Valley in 1966. Lines of men, women, and children passed beneath low, rolling clouds, beneath the red-and-black union flags and the flapping silk banners of the Virgin of Guadalupe. Their destination was the state capital, Sacramento, the city, Easter. They were private people praying in public. Here were the most compelling symbols of the pastoral past: life on the land (the farmworker); the flag, the procession in song (a people united, the village); the Virgin Mary (her consolation in sorrow).

Chávez wielded a spiritual authority that, if it was political at all, was not mundane and had to be exerted in large, priestly ways or it was squandered. By the late 1970s, Chávez had spent his energies in legislative maneuvers. His union got mixed up in a power struggle with the Teamsters. Criticized in the liberal press for allowing his union to unravel, Chávez became a quixotic figure; Gandhi without an India.

César Chávez was a folk hero. But the political example for my generation was Mayor Henry Cisneros of San Antonio. As a man of the city, Cisneros reflected our real lives in the America of *usted*. Cisneros attempted a reconciliation between the private and the public, between the family and the world. On the one hand, he belonged to the city. He spoke a metropolitan English, as well as Old Boy English; Cisneros spoke an international Spanish, as well as Tex-Mex. He chose to live in his grandfather's house on Monterey Street. The fiction was that he had never left home. Well, no—the fiction was that he had gone very far, but come home unchanged.

My mother saw Henry Cisneros twice on *60 Minutes*. My mother said she would vote for Cisneros for any office.

The career of Henry Cisneros magnified the dilemma of other Mexican Americans within that first generation of affirmative action. Had it not been for CBS News, my mother would never have heard of Henry Cisneros. Though his success was unique—though his talent is personal—my mother assumed that his career was plural, that he represented Mexican Americans because that is what he was—and that is what he was because he was the first. Groomed for leadership by an Ivy League college and by Democratic Party officials, Cisneros was then unveiled to the constituency he was supposed already to represent. He must henceforward use the plural voice on committees and boards and at conferences. We want. We need. The problem, in this case, is not with the candidate; it is with the constituency. Who are we? We who have been to Harvard? Or we who could not read English? Or we who could not read? Or we who have yet to take our last regard of the lemon tree in our mother's Mexican garden?

Politics can easily override irony. But, by the 1980s, the confusing "we" of Mexican Americanism was transposed an octave higher to the "we" of pan-American Hispanicism.

In the late 1980s, Henry Cisneros convened a conference of Hispanic leaders to formulate a national Hispanic political agenda.

Mexican Americans constituted the majority of the nation's Hispanic population. But Mexican Americans were in no position to define the latitude of the term "Hispanic"—the tumult of pigments and altars and memories there. "Hispanic" is not a racial or a cultural or a geographic or a linguistic or an economic description. "Hispanic" is a bureaucratic integer—a complete political fiction. How much does the Central American refugee have in common with the Mexican from Tijuana? What does the black Puerto Rican in New York have in common with the white Cuban in Miami? Those Mexican Americans who were in a position to speak for the group—whatever the group was—that is, those of us with access to microphones because of affirmative action, were not even able to account for our own success. Were we riding on some clement political tide? Or were we advancing on the backs of those who were drowning?

Think of earlier immigrants to this country. Think of the Jewish immigrants or the Italian. Many came, carefully observing Old World distinctions and rivalries. German Jews distinguished themselves from Russian Jews. The Venetian was adamant about not being taken for a Neapolitan. But to America, what did such claims matter? All Italians looked and sounded pretty much the same. A Jew was a Jew. And now America shrugs again. Palm trees or cactus, it's all the same. Hispanics are all the same.

I saw César Chávez again, a year ago, at a black-tie benefit in a hotel in San Jose. The organizers of the event ushered him into the crowded ballroom under a canopy of hush and tenderness and parked him at the center table, where he sat blinking. How fragile the great can seem. How much more substantial we of the ballroom seemed, the Mexican-American haute bourgeoisie, as we stood to pay our homage—orange women in fur coats, affirmative-action officers from cigarette companies, filmmakers, investment bankers, fat cats and stuffed shirts and bleeding hearts—stood applauding our little saint. César Chávez reminded us that night of who our grandparents used to be.

Then Mexican waiters served champagne.

Success is a terrible dilemma for Mexican Americans, like being denied some soul-sustaining sacrament. Without the myth of victimization—who are we? We are no longer Mexicans. We are professional Mexicans. We hire Mexicans. After so many years spent vainly thinking of ourselves as exempt from some common myth of America, we might as well be Italians.

■　■　■

Mexico's Children

I am standing in my sister's backyard.

They are away. The air is golden; the garden is rising green, but beginning to fall. There is my nephew's sandbox, deserted, spilled. And all his compliant toys fallen where he threw them off after his gigantic lovemaking. Winnie-the-Pooh. The waistcoated frog. Refugees of some long English childhood have crossed the Atlantic, attached themselves to the court of this tyrannical dauphin.

> *Aserrín aserrán*
> *Something something de San Juan . . .*

I can remember sitting on my mother's lap as she chanted that little faraway rhyme.

> *Piden pan. No les dan. . . .*

The rhyme ended with a little tickle under my chin. Whereas my nephew rides a cockhorse to Banbury Cross.

My youngest nephew. He has light hair; he stares at me with dark eyes. I think it is Mexico I see in his eyes, the unfathomable regard of the past, while ahead of him stretches Sesame Street. What will he know of his past, except that he has several? What will he know of Mexico, except that his ancestors lived on land he will never inherit?

The knowledge Mexico bequeaths to him passes silently through his heart, something to take with him as he disappears, like my father, into America.

■ ■ ■

In 1991, President Bush proposed the establishment of a free-trade consortium among North American "neighbors." In fact, the new idea derived from old Mother Mexico. It was Mother

Mexico, after all, who long ago mocked the notion of a border on the desert.

The United States shares with Mexico a two-thousand-mile connection—the skin of two heads. Everything that America wants to believe about himself—that he is innocent, that he is colorless, odorless, solitary, self-sufficient—is corrected, weighed upon, glossed by Mexico, the maternity of Mexico, the envy of Mexico, the grievance of Mexico.

Mexicans crossing the border are secret agents of matriarchy. Mexicans have slipped America a darker beer, a cuisine of *tú*. Mexicans have invaded American privacy to babysit or to watch the dying or to wash lipstick off the cocktail glasses. Mexicans have forced Southwestern Americans to speak Spanish whenever they want their eggs fried or their roses pruned. Mexicans have overwhelmed the Church—eleven o'clock masses in most Valley towns are Spanish masses. By force of numbers, Mexicans have taken over grammar-school classrooms. The Southwest is besotted with the culture of *tú*.

But Mexico was fooled by her own tragic knowledge of relationship. The desert is a tide. How could Mexico not have realized that tragedy would wash back on her, polluted with gringo optimism?

A young man leaves his Mexican village for Los Angeles in 1923. He returns one rainy night in 1925. He tells his family, next day he tells the village, that it is okay up there. The following spring, four village men accompany him back to L.A. They send money home. Mothers keep their sons' dollars in airtight jars, opening the jars only when someone is sick or someone is dying. The money is saturated with rumor.

Thus have Mexicans from America undermined the tranquillity of Mexican villages they thought only to preserve. The Mexican

American became a revolutionary figure, more subversive than a Chichimeca, more subversive than Pancho Villa.

In the 1970s, President Luis Echeverría invited planeloads of "Chicano leaders" to visit Mexico with the apparent goal of creating a lobby for the interests of Mexico modeled on the Israeli lobby. Perhaps the Chicano was the key to Mexico's future? The Chicano, after all, defied assimilation in the United States, or said he did. The Chicano sought to retain his culture, his mother tongue. In the 1980s, the government ministry in Mexico City announced a policy of reconciliation (*acercamiento*) regarding Mexican Americans.

By the 1980s, Mexican Americans were, on average, older, wealthier, better educated than the average Mexican; we also had fewer children. In the 1980s, the proud house of Mexico was crumbling, the economy was folding, the wealthy of Mexico had begun their exodus, following the peasant's route north. Along the border, Mexican towns inclined toward America and away from Mexico City. And from the North came unclean enchantments of the gringo—the black music, the blond breasts, the drugged eyes of tourists.

How much is the gum?

Mexico worries about her own. What influence shall she have? The village is international now. Most of the men have been north; many of the women, too. Have seen. Everyone has heard stories.

Mexico cannot hold the attention of her children. The average age of the country descends into adolescence. More than half of Mexico is under fifteen years of age. What is the prognosis for memory in a country so young?

For Mexico is memory. . . .

■   ■   ■

On the television, suspended from the ceiling over the bar, is Game Four of the World Series. I am sitting with five Mexicans at a restaurant in Mexico City. Presiding is a woman in her thirties, a curator of the National Anthropology Museum. Others are a filmmaker, a cameraman, a location scout. We are all connected by the making of a television film.

The woman is scolding me—not severely—for not being as fluent in Spanish as she is in English. She will do most of the talking.

She has traveled, studied in Europe. I forget now whether she knows the United States—probably—but she has met enough Mexican Americans to mimic their embarrassment concerning Spanish.

Poquito, poquito (a double entendre, holding an inch of air between the lacquered bulbs of her thumb and index finger).

Peut-être je devrais parler français avec vous, Richard.

We will disagree about everything, Mexico and I.

Do I really call myself a Catholic, she asks in reaction to nothing I have said. She, of course, hates the Church for what it has done to Mexico.

(Of course.)

Where do you get your ideas about Mexico? From Graham Greene? You have the opportunity to say something in public, and you go on and on about old churches and old mothers. You do a disservice with your reactionary dream of Mexico. Here, we are trying to progress. . . .

She has raised her own child—she has been married, oh yes —her own child is as free from the past as could be managed. Each generation must be free to discover its own identity, don't you think so. But, then, you have no children. Perhaps you have some Catholic malady, like sexual repression? She smiles.

I smile.

I feel I know them all; recognize the way their faces crease into smiles; recognize the ease of irony in a language so extravagant. Nothing is meant all that seriously, I suppose. They are speaking for my own benefit. They want to educate me.

I am not exactly bored, but I am demoralized.

They don't even seem like Mexicans. They are more like Americans of my generation. I would have avoided a dinner like this one, in a restaurant like this one, in California.

Do I have it all wrong? Was the Mexico I had imagined—the country of memory and faith—long past? Its curator a woman who reviles the past?

I lower my eyes. I say to Mexico, I say to my ice cubes:

I cannot understand you.

Do not pretend to understand me. I am but a figure of speech to you—a Mexican American.

What Richard needs to see, Alberto suggests, is . . . and then some Spanish name I don't catch. Titters all round.

We are drunk.

So, at one o'clock in the morning, we drive, five of us, crowded like clowns into a Volkswagen. I vote we go back to the hotel. The curator wants to listen to jazz. But the filmmaker is driving.

We end up at a nightclub on a quiet downtown street. The nightclub offers three kinds of therapy for sexual repression. We opt for the dinner theater. There is a small stage; twenty tables. Some Japanese businessmen at one table, some Mexicans at another. A drink costs a lot—ten American dollars.

A canned overture. Then two lines of dancers appear—"appear" cannot quite account for their corporeality. Twelve large vanilla flans, female; six samba shirts, male. The stage is so tiny the dancers must restrict their movements to the upper torso. After ten minutes of joust, a fog of dry ice is blasted from a funnel in the wings. The dancers fall to their knees and lift their arms to worship a tall, blond, goddessy woman who will sing of love.

The goddess's microphone is so revved up, her voice rides over our skulls like a metal lathe. Mid-routine, the goddess hesitates, evidently overcome with *nostalgie de la boue*. She descends two semicircular steps to ringside, her pink halo spilling after her. She stops at a table of Mexican men. She rests her hip against the shoulder of a man who has several rings on several of his fingers. He kisses her hand.

The filmmaker raises his arm, beckoning the goddess to our table, pointing at the crown of my head.

The goddess's eyes dart toward the filmmaker's hand. (There is a bank note caught like a butterfly between his fingers.) She lowers her forty lashes. Her pink penumbra shimmers tremulously; her lips curve upward. She begins to mash toward our table.

A cold hand caresses my cheek, a strong hand begins to tug at my necktie. The filmmaker giggles; the curator approves, lights a cigarette. The goddess makes sibilant remarks about me to the audience, little flatteries.

She begins to sing.

Tú. Tú. The song of the dove.

Tú the ruby pendant . . .

Suddenly she thrusts the microphone at my face.

The canned soundtrack rattles away in the distance but the air, suddenly bereft of the concussion of the goddess's voice, seems a world without love.

I decline.

The goddess laughs—a detonation, like claps of thunder. The air is alive again, freighted with angels. She picks up the lyric, looping the cord of the microphone into a coil. . . .

> *Vete pero no me olvides.*
> *Vete, amor,*
> *Amor de mi vida,*

Mexico's Children

Toma la rosa,
Tinta de vino. . . .

Violins edge into the track. The refrain. My cue. Again, the microphone is in my face.

The goddess looks infinitely bored. She wets her lips with her tongue, hacks up a little phlegm.

I sing.

I sing to her of my undying love and of rural pleasures. *Tú.* *Tú.* The ruby pendant. *Tú.* The lemon tree. The song of the dove. Breathed through the nose. Perched on the lips.

Anything to make her go away.

■ ■ ■

I wrote:

I once met an old woman in Mexico who looked lonelier than anyone I have ever seen. She was a beggar woman in a slum market in Mexico City. The aisles of the market were covered with canvas; on either side of these tent aisles hung chickens and flowers and pineapples for sale. Within the transept of the market, against a stone wall, the old woman kept her anchor-hold.

Hair grew out of her nose like winter breath. Her reply to every question was *no.* Nothing. Nobody. No husband. No sisters. No brother. Her only son dead.

If there was no one to claim her from the past, then she was unalterably separated from life. She lived in eternity. Even the poor neighborhood people, the poorest of the poor, could spare a few pesos for this mother of tragedy. People were in awe of her, for she was without grace, which in Mexico is children.

■ ■ ■

You stand around. You smoke. You spit. You are wearing your *two shirts, two pants, two underpants. Jesús says, if they chase* *you throw that bag down. Your plastic bag is your mama, all you*

77

have left; the yellow cheese she wrapped has formed a translucent rind; the laminated scapular of the Sacred Heart nestles flame in its cleft. Put it in your pocket. The last hour of Mexico is twilight, the shuffling of feet. A fog is beginning to cover the ground. Jesús says they are able to see in the dark. They have X-rays and helicopters and searchlights. Jesús says wait, just wait, till he says. You can feel the hand of Jesús clamp your shoulder, fingers cold as ice. Venga, corre. You run. All the rest happens without words. Your feet are tearing dry grass, your heart is lashed like a mare. You trip, you fall. You are now in the United States of America. You are a boy from a Mexican village. You have come into the country on your knees with your head down. You are a man.

■　■　■

I went to a village in the state of Michoacán, on the far side of Lake Chapala.

A dusty road leads past eucalyptus, past the cemetery, to the village. For most of the year the village is empty—nearly. There are a few old people, quite a few hungry dogs. The sun comes up; the sun goes down. Most of the villagers have left Mexico for the United States. January 23 is the feast day of the patron saint of the village, when the saint is accustomed to being rocked upon his hillock of velvet through the streets. On that day, the villagers—and lately the children of villagers—return. They come in caravans. Most come from Austin, Texas, from Hollister, California, and from Stockton, California. For a week every year, the village comes alive, a Mexican Brigadoon. Doors are unlocked. Shutters are opened. Floors are swept. Music is played. Beer is drunk. Expressed fragments of memory flow outward like cigarette smoke to tumble the dust of the dead.

Every night is carnival. Men who work at canneries or factories in California parade down the village street in black suits. Women who are waitresses in California put on high heels and evening gowns. The promenade under the Mexican stars becomes a celebration of American desire.

At the end of the week, the tabernacle of memory is dismantled, distributed among the villagers in their vans, and carried out of Mexico.

CHAPTER FOUR

In Athens Once

Palm Sunday. In the parking lot there is only silence and the scent of suntan lotion.

There is a turnstile.

Through which American tourists enter Mexico as at a state fair. Mexicans pass with the cardboard boxes they are using as suitcases. Some men are putting up palm trees. An old woman proffers sno-cones that look like bulbs of blood. She is wearing Gloria Vanderbilt jeans and jogging shoes.

I pass through the turnstile.

Already the sun feels older. Indian women sit on the pavement, their crafts spread out before them. There are wristbands of woven yarn, dolls made of ribbon, vibrant bushes of nodding paper poppies.

Hands and voices, beseeching eyes and rattling cups gather to surround me as I tread the gauntlet of pathetic enterprise.

CHICLETS. CHICLETOS.

Little girls not four years old sell Chiclets. Blind old women in blankets hawk Chiclets. Why? Why these little tiles of sugar jade? In Tijuana as in Bombay. A woman holding her baby with one arm will rattle a gross of Chiclets with her free hand. Five cents.

Tijuana, downtown. Taxi, mister? Taxi?

Chiclets, Taxi, are urgent questions in Tijuana, questions that soonest teach the visitor the custody of his eyes.

A boy sits on a ledge above the bay of taxis. He wears a cap —like a stage-urchin's cap. His face is wan and wolfen. His muzzle parts over sharpish teeth; his nostrils dilate to savor the crowd. Slowly he turns his face from side to side, as he would do if he were ravishing himself with a shaving brush.

He is surveying; his eyes are slits, appraising, rejecting; his eyes slide like searchlights, but do not rest on me.

The point of the United States is distinguishing yourself from the crowd. The point of Mexico is the crowd. Whatever happens in Tijuana, I caution myself, do not imagine you have been singled out. You have entered into the million.

Tijuana has a million, perhaps two million people. Tijuana will double in twelve years. Tijuana is the new Pacific city, larger than San Francisco or Seattle or Vancouver. Tijuana is larger than San Diego.

In its last advertised census, the Mexican government entered Tijuana's population as three-quarters of a million. Mexico City might have chosen to bid modestly as a way of dissuading attention from the swell along its northern border.

What intrigues us is that we cannot know. There is an uncountable *población flotante*. How can one number fluid shadows passing back and forth over the border, shadows whose business it is to elude any count?

Tijuana is several million lifetimes posing as one street, a metropolis crouched behind a hootchy-kootch curtain. Most Americans head for the tourist street called Avenida Revolución.

From the border you can share a cab for five bucks a head or you can walk along the Tijuana River, where you will see broken bottles and young men asleep on the grass. It is more fun, perhaps, to approach Revolución with adolescent preconceptions of lurid possibility. Marrakesh. Bangkok. For this you will need a cab. In the first place, where is he taking me? In the second place, cab drivers still offer male passengers *cualquier cosa* as a matter of form.

For all that, you are deposited safely when the cab driver announces, with a distracted wave of the hand, "El Main Street." El Main Street is what you'd expect of the region's fifth tourist attraction, after the San Diego Zoo, Sea World, some others. A Mexico ride. A quick shot of the foreign. Unmetered taxis. Ultramontane tongue. Disney Calcutta.

I am thinking of my first trip across: the late 1950s. We were on our way to visit relatives in Ensenada. We had driven all day from Sacramento in the blue DeSoto and we reached the border around midnight. I remember waking in the back seat. A fat Mexican in a brown uniform was making beckoning gestures in the light from our headlamps. This isn't Mexico, this isn't Mexico, my mother kept saying, clucking, smoothing. Tijuana is just a border town; you see the worst here. You'll see. I remember my father hunched forward at the wheel. The DeSoto was acting up. It was too late to drive any more. I remember a Saturday night, a big street full of scuffle and shadow: naked lights, persons stumbling, jeering. We found a motel by the bus station. We all slept on a double bed with a green velvet cover. We kept our clothes on. The air was heavy. Wet. I listened to faraway music. American music.

Mexico!

Most tourists come for the afternoon. Most tourists stay three or four hours, just between meals. After the shops, after the scolding sighs, after the bottled drinks, there is nothing to do but head back.

Another Sunday, 1961. I was spending a week with the Fahertys at Laguna Beach. Ernest Hemingway had shot himself in the mouth. (I was Hemingway's widow. I had read all his novels.) We were in Tijuana for the afternoon. We went to the new bullring by the sea. We sat in the expensive shade. On the opposite side were dark men in white shirts. Kim Novak was sitting a few rows in front of us. Pellets of blood struck the dust all afternoon. The Mexicans cheered the bull because the brave bull took so many thrusts of the matador's blade and yet refused to die. But the bull did die. The Mexicans cheered the matador. The matador passed a buzzing sachet—the ears of the bull—to Kim Novak while the band played a comic gavotte. Before it got dark, we drove back. Mr. Faherty had my birth certificate in his wallet, just in case. When an immigration officer questioned me over Mrs. Faherty's shoulder, I answered in a voice he accepted as having no accent; we were flagged forward. We stopped at Old Town in San Diego for a Mexican dinner.

Consider Tijuana from Mexico's point of view. Tijuana is farther away from Mexico City than any other city in Mexico. Tijuana is where Mexico comes to an end.

In Mexico City you will waste an afternoon if you go to bookstores looking for books about Tijuana. The clerk will scarcely conceal his amusement. (And what would be in a book about Tijuana?) People in Mexico City will tell you, if they have anything at all to say about Tijuana, that Tijuana is a city without history, a city without architecture, an American city. San Diego may worry about Mexican hordes crawling over the border. Mexico City worries about a cultural spill from the United States.

From prehistory, the North has been the problem. Mexico City (*la capital*) has been the platform from which all provincialism is gauged. From the North came marauding tribes, iconoclasts, destroyers of high Indian civilization. During the Spanish colonial era, the North was settled, even garrisoned, but scarcely civilized. In the nineteenth century, Mexico's northernmost territories were too far from the center to be defended against America's westward expansion. In after-decades, the North spawned revolutionaries and bandits, or these fled into the North and the North hid them well.

Beyond all the ribbon-cutting palaver about good neighbors, there remains an awesome distance of time. Tijuana and San Diego are not in the same historical time zone. Tijuana is poised at the beginning of an industrial age, a Dickensian city with palm trees. San Diego is a postindustrial city of high-impact plastic and despair diets. And palm trees. San Diego faces west, looks resolutely out to sea. Tijuana stares north, as toward the future. San Diego is the future—secular, soulless. San Diego is the past, guarding its quality of life. Tijuana is the future.

On the Mexican side there is flux, a vast migration, a camp of siege. On the Mexican side is youth, with bad skin or bad teeth, but with a naïve optimism appropriate to youth.

On the American side are petitions to declare English the official language of the United States; the Ku Klux Klan; nativists posing as environmentalists, blaming illegal immigration for freeway congestion. And late at night, on the radio call-in shows, hysterical, reasonable American voices say they have had enough. Of this or that. Of trampled flower beds. Of waiting in line or crowded buses, of real or imagined rudeness, of welfare.

In San Diego people speak of "the border" as meaning a clean break, the end of us, the beginning of them. In Mexican Spanish, the legality takes on distance, even pathos, as *la frontera*, meaning something less fixed, something more akin to the American "frontier." Whereas San Diego remains provincial and retiring, the intrusion of the United States has galvanized Tijuana to cosmopolitanism. There are seven newspapers in Tijuana; there is American television—everything we see they see. Central American refugees and southern California *turistas* cross paths in Tijuana. There are new ideas. Most worrisome to Mexico City has been the emergence of a right-wing idea, a pro-American politics to challenge the one-party system that has governed Mexico for most of this century.

Because the United States is the richer country, the more powerful broadcaster, Mexicans know more about us than we care to know about them. Mexicans speak of America as "the other side," saying they are going to *el otro lado* when they cross for work, legal or illegal. The border is real enough; it is guarded by men with guns. But Mexicans incline to view the border without reverence, referring to the American side as *el otro cachete*, the other buttock.

Traditionally, Mexican cities are centered by a town square or *zócalo*, on either side of which stand city hall and cathedral, counterweights to balance the secular with the eternal. Tijuana never had a *zócalo*. And, like other California cities, Tijuana is receding from its old downtown.

The new commercial district of Tijuana, three miles east of downtown, is called the Zona del Río. For several blocks within the Zona del Río, on grass islands in the middle of the Paseo de los Héroes, stand monuments to various of Mexico's heroes. There is one American (Abraham Lincoln) in a line that otherwise connects the good Aztec, Cuauhtémoc, to the victorious Mexican general, Zaragoza. With Kremlin-like dullness, these monuments were set down upon the city, paperweights upon a map. They are gifts from the capital, meant as reminders.

Prominent along the Paseo de los Héroes is Tijuana's Cultural Center, Mexico City's most insistent token of troth. Tijuana might better have done with sewers or streetlights, but in 1982 the Mexican government built Tijuana a cultural center, an orange concrete *bomba* in the brutal architectural idioms of the 1970s. The main building is a museum, very clean and empty during my visit, except for a janitor who trails me with a vacuum cleaner. Together we tread a ramp past fairly uninteresting displays of Mayan pottery, past folk crafts, past reproductions of political documents and portraits of Mexico's military heroes. The lesson to Tijuana is clear: she belongs to Mexico.

As the exhibits travel in time, south to north, the umbilical approach narrows to gossamer. We reach a display devoted to Tijuana's own history. We find a collection of picture postcards from the twenties, emblazoned in English with "Greetings from Old Mexico."

One sympathizes with the curator's dilemma. How does one depict the history of so unmonumental a city, a city occasioned by defeat and submission to the enemy's will?

The treaty ending the Mexican-American War ruled a longitudinal line between the Gulf of Mexico and the Pacific Ocean. For decades thereafter, Tijuana remained vacant land at the edge of the sea, an arid little clause dangling from Mexico's disgraced nineteenth century.

No one in Tijuana is able to fix for me the derivation of the name of the place. Some say it is an Indian name. Some think the town was named for a woman who lived in a shack at the turn of the century, a Mexican Ma Kettle known in the region as Tía Juana.

Mexico City tried to dispose of the name in 1925. By an act of Mexico's congress, Tijuana was proclaimed to be Ciudad Zaragoza. A good name. A patriot's name. The resolution languished in a statute book on a shelf in Mexico City, two thousand miles away.

■ ■ ■

Monday of Holy Week. On the side streets of the Zona Norte, by the old bus station, Mexican men loiter outside the doors of open bars. From within come stale blasts of American rock. Is this all that is left of the fleshpots of T.J.?

We are a generation removed from that other city, the city generations of American men mispronounced as "Tee-ah-wanna," by which they named an alter-ego American city, a succubus that could take them about as far as they wanted to go. At the turn of the century, when boxing was illegal in San Diego, there was blood sport in Tijuana. There were whores and there was gambling and there was drink.

Mexico spends millions to lure Americans toward the sun; Mexico's allure has for a longer time been as the dark, a country of nuance and mascara.

Civic leaders in Tijuana are ashamed of the lewd tattoo on the reputation of their city. Progressives refer to the past as "the dark legend." Tijuana would rather you noticed the daytime city— the office towers, the industrial parks.

Traditionally, Mexicans eat at about the time Americans get ready for bed. Mexicans move as naturally and comfortably in the dark as cats or wolves or owls do. Mexicans take their famous promenade around the plaza at night, meet and gossip beneath the lamppost. Mexicans get drunk and sing like cats beneath the moon.

Traditionally, Mexicans have been ridiculed by Americans as people who sleep the day away. The figure on the ceramic ashtray, the figure that forms the bookend—the Mexican figurine is forever taking his siesta, propped against a cactus, shaded by his sombrero. Mexicans are always late or, refusing to be circumscribed by time, they resort to *mañana*. *Mañana* is the Mexican's gloss on the light of day. *Mañana*, by definition, will never come. *Mañana* intends to undo all the adages of the English language. Waste not, want not. Don't put off till tomorrow. A stitch in time.

Do you linger over the figurine? Today, for you—eight dollars.

Mexican cynicism is an aspect of the Mexican habit of always seeking the shade. Nothing is what it seems in the light of day. The Mexican politician wears dark glasses. He says one thing. Everyone understands the reverse to be true. The traffic citation can be commuted with a bribe. The listed price is subverted with a wink.

What is money between friends? Six dollars?

Americans distrust Mexican shading. The genius of American culture and its integrity come from fidelity to the light. Plain as day, we say. Happy as the day is long. Early to bed, early to rise. Up and at 'em. American virtues are daylight virtues: honesty, plain style. We say yes when we mean yes and no when we mean no. Americans take short shrift from sorrow, reassuring one another that tomorrow is another day or time heals all wounds or things will look better in the morning.

A teenage policeman says: "The gringos find our downtown so ugly? They were the ones who made it." Which is true enough, though the lustier truth is that Mexican cynicism met American hypocrisy in Tijuana. Mexico lay down and the gringo paid in the morning.

At its best and worst, Mexico is tolerant. Spanish Catholicism bequeathed to Mexico an assumption of Original Sin. Much in life is failure or compromise. The knowledge has left Mexico patient as a desert, and tolerant of corruptions that have played upon her surface. Public officials tread a path to corruption, just as men need their whores. *No importa*. Mexico manages to live.

The intimate life, the family life—abundant and eternal—is

In Athens Once

Mexico's consolation against the knowledge of sin. *Mamacita*, sainted Mama, stokes her daughter's purity, which is a jewel betokening the family's virtue. A woman of Tijuana tells me she was never permitted by her parents within two blocks of Avenida Revolución. Young ladies of Tijuana required *dueñas* long after Mexico City had discontinued the habit.

I am chaperoned through the city by an official from the Comité de Turismo y Convenciones. Her English is about as bad as my Spanish. We stroll the Avenida Revolución, recently beautified —wider sidewalks, new blighted trees. There, says my hostess, where the Woolworth's now stands (where disinterested hag beggars squat, palms extended over their heads), used to be the longest bar in the world. And over there, beyond the blue tourist bus (which is being decanted by a smiling guide with a very wide tie), is the restaurant where two Italian brothers named Cardini created the Caesar salad back in the twenties.

In Tijuana, as in Las Vegas, another city constructed on sand, and almost as old, history is a matter of matchbook covers and cocktail napkins.

Tijuana used to be very glamorous, promises my companion from the Comité de Turismo y Convenciones. We are considering a building (a trade school) where the Casino de Agua Caliente once stood. She thinks. She herself is from Guadalajara. Anyway, all the famous movie stars used to come down.

Among the however many million volumes in the library at the University of California in San Diego there is one green book about Tijuana—not thick—a history written by John Price, an American professor. The book includes photographs of the Casino de Agua Caliente in the twenties—Moorish architecture, shadows of palm trees, silver sky.

In the same green book, a photograph survives of Sheilah Graham, she on a mule; Tijuana sombrero; hilarious. Her attendant Joseph is none other than the tarnished high priest of the twenties, F. Scott Fitzgerald. Both look foolish in ways they hadn't intended.

San Diego changed first. By the 1940s, Prohibition was over and Tijuana had lost some of its glamorous utility. During the war, Tijuana was relegated to the sailor's rest. From those war years, a Venusberg lore has passed from American fathers to sons, together with prescriptions against infection. Wet dreams advance on the cackle of a lewd horn: a blinking neon cactus; a two-quart margarita; and any of several more lurid images, like the demoiselles who can pick quarters off the table without using their hands.

Tijuana is now off-limits to the U.S. Navy between 8:00 P.M. and dawn. The press officer at the San Diego Naval Station tells me sailors have been harassed by the Tijuana police.

But if you want pornography, go to San Diego, the Mexicans say. And you won't see people selling drugs on the streets of Tijuana. When the Mexican woman wants an abortion, she crosses the border, the Mexicans say.

There is the father in Tijuana who worries that his teenage son is living under the radiant cloud of American pop culture, its drugs, its disrespect, its despair. San Diego's morning paper quotes officials in Washington concerning corrupt Mexican officials and an unchecked northern flow of drugs. Washington does not credit America's hunger for drugs with raising drug lords south of the border.

Mexico does not deny any of it—well, some—but Mexico has a more graceful sense of universal corruption. What Mexico comprehends is a balance between supply and demand. The Mexican comprehends public morality as a balance—the ethereal parts of any balanced thing rise by virtue of the regrettable ballast. The border, for instance. For Mexicans, the border is not that rigid

Puritan thing, a line. (Straight lines are unknown in Mexico.) The border, like everything else, is subject to supply and demand. The border is a revolving door.

U.S. Immigration officials describe the San Ysidro border crossing as "the busiest in the world." If U.S. Immigration officials counted forty million people passing through the San Ysidro border crossing last year, Mexico assumes a two-way street. So: Tijuana had the same forty million visitors last year. Tijuana bills itself "the most visited city in the world." It becomes, in a way, the Mexican's joke on the gringo's paranoia, his penchant for numbers, his fear of invasion or contamination.

The trouble with gringo tourists, the Mexican hotel manager confides, is their temerity abroad. The water! Nothing wrong with the water, the Mexican says; I drink it all day. The gringos won't swim in the pool or sing in the shower or suck on the ice. They pick at their food. Is it safe? Is it clean?

America has long imagined itself clean, crew-cut, ingenuous. We are an odorless, colorless, accentless, orderly people, put upon and vulnerable to the foreign. Aliens are carriers of chaos —Mexicans are obviously carriers of chaos—their backs are broken with bundles of it: gray air, brown water, papacy, leprosy, crime, diarrhea, white powders, and a language full of newts and cicadas.

Mexico does not say it publicly but Mexico perceives America as sterile, as sterilizing, as barren as the nose of a missile. "Don't drink the water in Los Angeles," goes the joke, "it will clean you out like a scalpel." Because Americans are barren by choice, Americans are perceived by Mexico as having relinquished gravity. Within the porticos of the great churches of Mexico are signs reminding visitors to behave with dignity. The signs are in English.

Seasoned visitors from southern California pass right on through

Tijuana, as through some final entanglement with history. Campers and jeeps head south into the vacant depths of Baja—California's newest, unofficial national park. Just as an earlier generation used Tijuana to refresh its virtue, so once again Californians use Mexico as an opposite planet. As pollution settles over Orange County, Baja California is prized for its pristine desert, its abiding austerity. Even so, southern California is busy re-creating itself on the far coasts of Baja, building condos, negotiating time-share beach houses in subdivisions with street names like Vista Mar.

Gingerly I am steered through the inedible city by my hostess from the Comité de Turismo y Convenciones. Street vendors offer unclean enchantments, whirling platters of melon and pineapple, translucent candies, brilliant syrups, charcoaled meats, black and red. All are tempting, all inedible. Mexicans bite and lick and chew and swallow. I begin to feel myself a Jamesian naïf who puzzles and perspires and will not dare.

"The usual visit, then, three or four hours?"

I notice my hostess is surreptitiously consulting her wristwatch. I'm spending the week, I tell her. I admit to her that I am visiting Tijuana by day, sleeping in San Diego at night.

Ah.

We stop at a café. She offers me something to drink. A soft drink, perhaps?

No, I say.

¿Cerveza?

But suddenly I fear giving offense. I notice apothecary jars full of improbably colored juices, the colors of calcified paint.

Maybe some jugo, please.

Offense to whom? That I fear drinking Mexico?

A waiter appears from stage left with a tall glass of canary yellow.

In Athens Once

Ah.

We are all very pleased. It's lovely today. I put the glass to my lips.

But I do not drink.

■ ■ ■

Tuesday of Holy Week. A noisy artificial waterfall outside my window at the Inter-Continental Hotel in San Diego is designed to drown out the noise of traffic. The traffic report on the radio posts a thirty-minute delay at the San Ysidro border crossing. Children of upper-class Tijuana are crossing into San Diego for school. Mexicans with green cards are heading to their American jobs. From the American side, technicians, engineers, and supervisors are heading for jobs in Tijuana. The thirty-minute delay is in both directions.

It was in the nineteenth century that American entrepreneurs began reaching into Mexico for cheap labor to build California. In good times, most Americans approved the arrangement, hard work for low wages. But whenever the economy dipped, Mexicans slid down the board. They bumpered up in Tijuana.

Leo Chávez, an anthropologist in San Diego, tells me there is nothing inexplicable about illegal immigration. America lured the Mexican worker; America established the financial dependency that today America relegates to realms of tragedy. Sons following fathers north; it became a rite of passage—"like going to college," Chávez observes. Tijuana is crowded today with such families. Papa crosses over into the twenty-first century; Mama raises the kids at the edge of the nineteenth century.

Tijuana is not Mayhew's London; there are no dark naves of Victorian mills. You see smoke on the horizon. It turns out to be a bonfire on a vacant lot. That this is an optimistic city is apparent mainly in the traffic.

One sees few pedestrians (few sidewalks). Dogs roam dusty

lots. In Colonia Libertad some teenagers gather about a car without wheels. If the car had wheels they wouldn't be there.

All the adages about California cities—suburbs in search of a center, no there there—describe Tijuana also. Tijuana is a *municipio*, something like an American county. Tijuana extends about twenty-five miles south and east from its old downtown to include surrounding townships. All are united by one mayor and a single ambition. The ambition of Tijuana is American dollars.

In the lobby of the Lucerna Hotel, I see the sort of family one sees in only two or three hotels in Mexico City. Father with a preoccupied look and thin watch; mother elegant, glacially indulgent of her three children, who squirm under the watchful eye of an Indian nanny.

The word for money in Tijuana is *maquiladora*. *Maquiladora* means assembly plant. Twenty years ago, the Mexican government established a duty-free zone along the border, permitting foreign companies to transport parts and raw materials into Mexico. The assembled products could then be shipped to the United States for consumption.

Most of the foreign-owned assembly plants are in new, quietly marked buildings on the east side of town wherein thousands of doomed señoritas spin dreams of love and idleness as their nimble fingers assemble the detritus of modern civilization. The manager of one assembly plant by the airport predicts that all of Mexico will soon look like Tijuana. No one looks up as we pass. In a corner, beneath a metallic template marking the exit, is a shrine to Our Lady of Guadalupe.

Tijuana is an industrial park on the outskirts of Minneapolis. Tijuana is a colony of Tokyo. Tijuana is a Taiwanese sweatshop. Tijuana is a smudge beyond the linden trees of Hamburg. There is complicity between businessmen—hands across the border—and shared optimism.

In Athens Once

On the San Diego side businessmen speak of "mutual benefit," by which is meant profit from the proximity of technology and despair. What capitalism has in mind for Tijuana depends upon the availability of great numbers of the Mexican poor; depends upon the poor remaining poor. For their labor Mexicans are paid Mexican wages. Mexico's daily wage is America's hourly wage. Some such deal involving cheap labor has doubtless brought Papa to meet his Japanese counterpart in the lobby of the Lucerna Hotel.

A second border crossing has opened at Otay Mesa. In my rented car I traverse the rust-colored fields. I look to left and to right, trying to imagine the industrial Camelot.

Yes, freighted trucks will pass emptied trucks back and forth across the border. Yes, profit will rise from the interaction of stable with unstable economies. But this time America will not be able to get rid of Tijuana once we have done with her poor. Tokyo can. The Koreans are only renting Tijuana for the season. But the anticipatory, desperate city massing beyond the cyclone fence is not going to dissipate into ether at the sound of the five o'clock whistle.

The poor can live on far less than justice. But the poor have a half-life to outlast radium.

Back at the Inter-Continental Hotel, Twelfth Night is in progress. American businessmen in baggy swimsuits sit around the noisy waterfall reading about Japan. A woman of profoundly indeterminate age lopes by—spandex, sunglasses, earphones. An aging kiddo in a bikini stands on his head while a golden Frisbee slices up to catch the fading light of California.

■ ■ ■

Spy Wednesday. Mexico would rather schedule a sucker-appointment than seem to deny a journalist's request. I phone a city official in Tijuana. His secretary is at my service (*a sus*

95

órdenes). She will phone me right back to confirm the appointment; no one calls back. I rush in for a ten-thirty meeting with Señor B. or Licenciado R. His secretary is desolated to have to tell me that Señor B. or Licenciado R. is at a "mixer" in San Diego.

Information in an authoritarian society is power. In Mexico, power accumulates as information is withheld.

Or else I get an interview with a Mexican official and find that even the most innocuous rag of fact is off the record, *por favor*. The professor from the Colegio de la Frontera stops mid-sentence to crane his neck across the table whenever my pen touches paper.

I sit on an oversize sofa in the outer office of a Mexican big shot, studying his airbrushed photograph on the wall. I wait thirty minutes, an hour, before I pad back to the secretary's desk. Señor B. was called away to Mexicali by the governor two days ago. Everything is so upset. Then the radiant smile, the dawning of an explanation: This is Easter Week, señor.

■　■　■

Holy Thursday. I am going to La Casa de los Pobres, a kitchen for the poor run by Franciscan nuns. Evidently La Casa is well known, because the taxi driver doesn't ask for directions.

As I sit in the back seat of the taxi, lulled by sensations of perambulation, I nevertheless attempt to memorize the route. I have seen worse neighborhoods than the ones we drive through. Detroit is worse. East London. But this is Mexico. Because Mexico is brown and I am brown, I fear being lost in Mexico.

When I get out of the cab, I am in a crowd; I am forced by the crowd through a gate, and into a courtyard the color of yellow cake. I can smell coffee, cinnamon, eggs, frijoles.

I look around for Tom Lucas, a Jesuit priest from Berkeley who invited me here. All that I know about Tom Lucas I have learned from him over lunch at Chez Panisse. The man I recognize in the kitchen at La Casa is speaking Spanish with three Mexican nuns.

At eleven o'clock, groceries are handed out. The poor form a line; everyone in line holds a number. Volunteers are assigned stations behind a bank of tables. What a relief it is, after days of dream-walking, invisible, through an inedible city, to feel myself actually doing something, picking up something to hand to someone. Thus Mexico's poor pass through my hands. Most women bring their own plastic bags. The bags are warm and smell of sweat as I fill them with four potatoes, two loaves of bread, two onions, a cup of pinto beans, a block of orange cheese. I thank each of the Mexicans. This baffles them, but they nod.

In the afternoon, Tom Lucas takes me with him to the Colonia Flores Magón, a poor section of Tijuana, not the poorest, considering the hills are green and there is a fresh wind blowing.

Even before our pickup comes to a full stop, doors have started to open. First one woman comes out of a house, then several more women come out of their houses, then more women are descending the hillsides.

"*Padrecito,*" the call is tossed among the women playfully. Most of these women are in their late twenties, most have several children.

Would it be possible, Father, for you to bless my house?

In the seminary Father Lucas may have imagined an activist, perhaps even a revolutionary ministry. He discourages the women from kissing his hand. Yes, he says, yes he will bless houses.

Some houses are solidly built of concrete blocks. Some houses resemble California suburban houses of the 1960s. Some houses have dirt floors and walls of tin. Some houses are papered with the *Los Angeles Times*. In front of many houses are tubs of soapy water.

People have heard there is a priest. Together we walk toward a neighborhood park—*padrecito,* the mothers, the children, the barking dogs. An altar is already set up. There are white carnations in coffee cans. White light bulbs have been strung in the branches of an olive tree. This is Holy Thursday, the commemoration of the Last Supper and the institution of the Eucharist. Twelve teenage boys have been rounded up by their mothers to slouch at the altar, dressed in bathrobes and sheets to impersonate the Twelve Apostles. They grin stupidly at one another as Father Lucas washes their feet according to the ancient rite of divine humility.

A yellow fog is coming in over the hills behind us. Overhead a jetliner is pushing up from Tijuana International, slowly turning left, south, toward Guadalajara and Mexico City. Some people in the crowd seem bored, grow restless. Thirty yards behind the altar, teenagers are playing basketball.

In the rear of our pickup are cartons of day-old junk pastries from a San Diego bakery. My job will be to distribute these to the children after mass. When I hear my cue from the altar—*In the name of the Father, and of the Son, and of the Holy Ghost*—I climb over the tailgate and wait there with my arms folded, my legs spread, like a temple guardian. Then Father Lucas instructs parents to bring their children to the truck for a special treat.

Five or six children come forward. All goes well for less than a minute. The crowd has slowly turned away from the altar, blessing itself. Now the crowd advances zombielike against the truck. I'm afraid the children will be crushed. *¡Cuidado!* Silent faces regard me with incomprehension. An old hag with chicken skin on her arms grabs for my legs—extravagant swipes, lobsterlike, or as if she were plucking a harp—trying to reach the boxes behind me.

I fling the pastries over outstretched hands to the edge of the crowd. I throw package after package until there are no more. The crowd hesitates, draws back.

I sit in the truck for an hour waiting for Father Lucas to finish with them. Some bratty kids hang around the truck, trying to get my attention. I watch instead some old men as they stretch their hands toward a bonfire.

Around seven o'clock, Father Lucas places the unused consecrated wafers inside the glove compartment. The truck bounces on dusty roads. There are few streetlights, no street names. After several dead ends, we are lost. Down one road, we come upon a pack of snarling dogs. Backing up, we come near to backing off a cliff. Once more we drive up a hill. Then Tom recognizes a house. A right turn, a left. The road takes on gravel. At the base of the canyon we see the highway leading to Ensenada. In the distance, I can see the lights of downtown Tijuana, and beyond, the glamorous lights that cradle San Diego Bay. It is a sight I never expected to see with Mexican eyes.

■ ■ ■

Good Friday. A gray afternoon in Chula Vista, a few miles north of the border. The U.S. Border Patrol station is Spanish colonial in design. The receptionist is Mexican-American. On the wall of the press office is a reproduction of an Aztec stone calendar.

There is a press office.

The PR officer says he is glad to have us—journalists—"helps in Washington if the public can get a sense of the scope of the problem."

The PR officer is preoccupied with a West German film crew. They were promised a ride in a helicopter. Where is the helicopter? Two journalists from a Tokyo daily—with five canvas bags of camera equipment between them—lean against the wall, their arms folded. One of them brings up his wrist to look at his watch. A reporter from Chicago catches my sleeve, Did I hear about last night?

?

Carload of Yugoslavs caught coming over.

The Japanese reporter who is not looking at his watch is popping Cheezits into his mouth. The Border Patrol secretary has made an error. She has me down as a reporter for *American Farmer*. Apologies. White-out. I . . . *agree to abide by any oral directions given to me during the operation by the officer in charge of the unit*. Having signed the form, I get introduced to a patrolman who will be my guide to the night. He is about my age and of about my accent, about my color, about my build.

We drive out. Almost immediately the patrolman stops his truck on a cliff. He hands me his binoculars. In the foreground are the last two miles of the United States of America, scrub canyon; and beyond, Tijuana—the oldest neighborhood—Colonia Libertad; and beyond, the new commercial skyline; and beyond, the sovereign hills of Mexico.

Somewhere up in those Mexican hills, Father Lucas is leading a Good Friday service. The Crucifixion will be re-enacted. There will be a procession. The man elected to play Christ will drag a pine cross up a gravel path. At the top of the hill, Christ will be strapped to his cross; the cross will be hoisted. Cristo will stand upon a pedestal on the upraised cross for about half an hour. He will hear only the wind in his ears as, below him, the crowd prays.

I have elected to spend the afternoon among the chariots and the charioteers. I raise the binoculars to my eyes. Throughout the canyon are people—men, in twos and threes. Down below, perhaps three miles away, is a level plain called the soccer field, because men who will cross the border often pass the time before dark playing soccer. There are pale fires—old women cooking chickens to sell. A Brueghel-like wintry haze attends the setting of the sun.

Ten yards below us, a man, a boy, sits cross-legged by a fire, reading a book. He looks up at us, but seems not to be aware of us. His lips move. He looks down to his book. He is memorizing.

"It's almost always a learn-English book," the patrolman says.

Around six o'clock, the wind comes up, the sky begins to flap like a tent. I can see the lights of rush-hour traffic at the San Ysidro border crossing. By now we are cruising a ragged cyclone fence. Some Mexican kids peek through, smiling.

"Sometimes people throw rocks," says the patrolman.

Again we are on the mesa. It is dark. Helicopters drag blades of light through the canyons, rendering the crooked straight and the rough places plain. The patrolman confides he is using a code on his radio to alert his fellows that he carries Press. My tour will remain pretty much *son et lumière*.

We come upon a posse of border patrolmen preparing to ride through the canyon on horseback. I get out of the truck; ask questions; pet the horses in the dark—prickly, moist, moving in my hand. An officer we meet obliges me with his night-vision telescope, from which I am encouraged to take a sample of the night. He calls me sir. He invites me so close to his chin, I smell cologne as I peer through the scope. It is as though I am being romanced at a cowboy cotillion.

The night is alive. The night is green as pond water, literally crawling with advancing lines of light.

A VIP shuttle van speeds down a hill Stateside; comes to a stop twenty feet beyond our truck. A side door slides open; five men in suits emerge. We stand together on a bluff, silent, grave as Roman senators in a Victor Mature movie. A woman remains inside the van. Petulant? Cold? I can just see the outline of her flared hairdo.

An hour later, we are parked. The patrolman turns off the lights of the truck—"Back in a minute"—a branch scrapes the door as he rolls out of the cab to take a piss. Brush crackles beneath his receding steps. I am alone.

Who? Who is out there?

Dishwashers, gardeners, field workers. Faces I have seen all my life. No big deal. There are *pollos*—inexperienced travelers in Tijuana slang. Women are *pollos*. Children are *pollos*. Central Americans with all their money stuffed in their shoes are *pollos*.

Pollos have predators. One hand covers your mouth. Other hands tug at your clothing, swift to harvest your poor life. A kick to your belly, a jerk of your hair, the blade at your throat.

The cab lights up. The patrolman slides in. We drive again. In the dark, I do not separate myself from the patrolman's intention.

The patrolman has cut his headlights. The truck accelerates, pitches off the rutted road, banging, the slam of a rock, faster, ignition is off, the truck is soft-pedaled to a stop in the dust; the patrolman is out like a shot. The cab light is on. I sit exposed. I can't hear. I decide to follow. I leave my door open as the patrolman has done. There is a boulder in the field. Is that it? The patrolman is barking in Spanish. His flashlight is trained on the boulder. He traces his beam along the grain, as though he is untying a knot. Three men and a woman stand up. The men are young. Maybe sixteen. The youngest is shivering. He makes a fist. He looks down. The woman is young, too. Or she could be the mother. Her legs are thin. She wears a man's wristwatch. They come from somewhere. And somewhere—San Diego, Sacramento—someone is waiting for them.

The patrolman tells them to take off their coats and their shoes; throw them in a pile. Another truck rolls up.

In Athens Once

As a journalist I am allowed to come close. I can even ask questions.

There are no questions.

You can take your pictures, the patrolman says.

I stare at the faces. They stare at mine. To them I am not bearing witness; I am part of the process of being arrested. I hold up my camera; their eyes swallow the flash—a long tunnel, leading back.

Chula Vista. The streets are quiet. The patrolman has his eye on a taxi idling by the phone booth outside 7-Eleven. ("They call for a taxi to take them into L.A.—anywhere from fifty bucks.") Ignition. Lights. As we hurl forward, the taxi tears away. In front of the phone booth a solitary man, about fifty years old, makes one slow turn in our spotlight. He wears a Dodgers cap to make himself invisible. He smiles as the patrolman gets out of the truck. He extends his arms toward the patrolman, as a somnambulist would. Then he bows his head and delivers over his spirit.

Most people arrested are docile. They know the rules favor them. They will be taken to a detention center, which is a room full of Mexicans watching Johnny Carson. They will waive their right to a trial. In the cool of the morning they will be driven back to the border.

■ ■ ■

Holy Saturday. "Show me Tijuana, what you think I should see." Four times during the week, with four different guides, I am given more or less the identical tour. Downtown *muy rápido*. Then leisurely south to Rosarito Beach, where the gringos have built condos ("like illegal aliens," according to native wit). Then backtrack to Rodríguez Dam. The gray international airport. The smoked-glass towers of the Fiesta Americana Hotel. Then a slow sweep around the Tijuana Country Club and golf course, climbing toward the grandest houses in town.

Days of Obligation

This is the section of Tijuana known as Chapultepec. The name pays homage to a fashionable district of Mexico City. Here architectural styles derive less from Spanish-colonial memory, scarce in Tijuana, than from international eclecticism—Cinderella château, California Bauhaus. One is not rebuffed by the tall walls characteristic of the colonial high style of Mexico. One is rewarded, instead, with picture windows. The houses are constructed facing the United States.

Shall we stop the car? Get out for a look?

Think of the Joad family's earlier view of the paradisaical Central Valley. Then think, many generations before the Joads, of Spanish galleons sailing up the Pacific Coast. California was first seen by the Spaniards—as through Asian eyes. Let this view from the hills of Tijuana stand as the modern vision of California.

My final tour of the city ends as an afterthought (because my host wants to buy some liquor for Easter) at the Río Plaza, an American-style shopping mall. Walking through the parking lot in front of Sears, I think I might be in Stockton. Once inside the mall, I realize I have stumbled upon the *zócalo* of Tijuana.

Overfragranced crowds of Mexican teenagers are making their *paseo* between the record shop and the three-theater *cine*-complex. I pause to get my bearings and to measure the proportions of this city within a city. I am reminded of the model of an Aztec metropolis in a Mexico City museum; fancy leads me further to seek the Templo Mayor. I turn the corner and there it is, belching incense and idolatry, pulling like a magnet—the great temple of middle-class desire—a supermarket called Commercial Mexicana. Commercial is bigger, more crowded—happier—more prodigiously stocked than any supermarket I have ever seen. The meat counter ranges from beef intestines to translucent, delicate, slimy fish. To snake. To lung. To snout. To hoof. There are caldrons of congealed brown *mole*; there are ceiling-high pyramids of six-packs, eight-packs, econo-packs, super-savers. Boxes of detergent and bags of metallic-looking candies and packages of toilet paper come in gigantic Mexican "family" sizes never seen in America. There are luxuries, conveniences, necessities —everything. Everything! The only souvenir of the New World I decide to bring back with me are five bottles of Liquid Paper correction fluid, because I can't believe the price.

■ ■ ■

Easter Sunday. Father Lucas phones me before I check out of my hotel in San Diego. The beer-belly who played Jesus refused, when the time came, to take off his shirt, so they had to hoist him up like Christ the King in a gold sweatshirt. By and by, Christ relented; the shirt came off. And somehow it all worked. Tom wishes I had been there. I should have heard the sound the cross made as it was dragged across the gravel. Jesus brought along some cronies to chat with him while he was on the cross. I should have seen the devout old ladies, the awestruck children, "the way it must have been in Jerusalem—a curious mixture of mood."

Tom spent most of Saturday looking for a coffin for a baby. The parents were too poor to afford more than a shoe box. "Even the children here know about death. Brother lifts baby sister up so she can have a peek into the coffin." For once, says Tom, for his own sake, he was glad of the book, the consolation of liturgy.

Tom says he is going back to the Colonia Flores Magón to celebrate Easter mass in the park. Do I want to come along?

I do not.

I do not tell him I have made plans to meet friends for brunch in La Jolla. I put down the receiver. Not for the first time I am glad of the complaisancies of the Inter-Continental Hotel.

The theme of city life is the theme of difference. People living separately, simultaneously. In all the great cities of the world, as in all the great novels, one senses this. The village mourns in unison, rejoices as one. But in the city . . . In Athens once, I remember sitting in an outdoor café, amid sun and cheese and flies, when a hearse with a picture window slid by, separated from its recognizing mourners by rush-hour traffic—an intersecting narrative line—which, nevertheless, did not make mourners of us, of the café.

Taken together as one, Tijuana and San Diego form the most fascinating new city in the world, a city of world-class irony. Within thirty minutes of the checkout desk at the Inter-Continental, I am once more on the Avenida Revolución, where shopkeepers are sweeping sidewalks, awaiting an onslaught of *turistas*.

Inside Tijuana's aquamarine cathedral I sit behind a family of four—a father, a mother, a boy, a girl. They have thick hair. At the elevation of the host, each holds up a tiny homemade cross of stapled palm leaves.

Less than an hour later, I am in La Jolla.

Where friends want to know what I think of Tijuana. I shrug. (I imagine the dead baby packed away in orchids.) It's there, I say.

But what I want to say is that Tijuana is here. It has arrived. Silent as a Trojan horse, inevitable as a flotilla of boat people, more confounding in its innocence, in its power of proclamation, than Spielberg's most pious vision of a flying saucer.

Later in the afternoon, in a cold spring wind, we walk around Louis Kahn's concrete Salk Institute, admiring the way California wanted to imagine its future. We walk on toward the beach. The sky has filled with hang gliders, drifting, silently drifting, like wondrous red- and blue-winged angels, over the sea.

CHAPTER FIVE

The Missions

Part One: Father of California

Two tow-headed teenagers at the Texaco station do not seem
to know what I want when I ask for directions to the mission.
One of them thinks there is something like that over by the football
stadium.

*There is a parking lot, gravel. There is a bank of patulous cactus
on which someone has carved his initials. The main door of the
church is locked—ENTER THROUGH GIFT SHOP—in the lettering
printshops call Lombardic. There is an old woman behind the
counter, a volunteer. Admission is one or two dollars. Brochures
are free. The cat is somewhere—asleep in a puddle of sun, on a
casement, or preening herself in a doorway.*

*The "tour" begins with the museum, objects that have fallen
through time. Tightly woven baskets with the black tracery we
recognize as California Indian. Stone mortars. Arrowheads plucked
from dry creek beds by boys in 1910.*

Next come the Spanish and Mexican rooms: portraits of colonial

107

governors; proclamations, deeds. The missals and the vestments belonged to the mission priests. Chalices. Monstrances. Candelabra. Shards of European crockery. Eyeglasses. Medicine bottles. Quills.

Then the American rooms: The oils of itinerant painters. Early photographs of mission ruins. Photographs of Irish priests and California civic leaders.

Everywhere the smoke-darkened Mexican paintings of Spanish saints.

There is a cloister. There is a glistening Arabic garden. (Oranges, olives, dates, figs.) Or there is a dusty close bordered by cactus, lit by butterflies.

The mission was not only a church, it was a living community. Here a blacksmith shop, there soldiers were garrisoned. This was the kitchen—plastic chiles, festoons of garlic, a gum wrapper tossed in an iron pot.

These long rooms are the rooms where the padres taught the Indians the agriculture of Europe or the music of Europe or the mythology of Europe.

The church is dark and cool. There is a used quality to mission churches that seems friendly, provided one is on easy terms with Catholic iconography. There are wooden saints—tragic dolls dressed in velvets and laces. For the most part, the missions feature no architectural detail beyond beamed ceilings and high, recessed windows. They are, however, wonderfully gaudy. The wanted details were painted on the walls by Indians imagining Europe: pillars of marble, arches, niches, draperies, swags, balustrades, vines, clouds, shells, suns, stars, the eye of God. What strikes the eye of the beholder is a hybrid of imperfect European memory—the loosening of rigid perspective—compensated by the exuberance of necessity.

There is a cemetery behind the church. Spanish names on stone obelisks. A plain wooden tablet must stand for the hundreds of Indians "buried at this site."

A sprinkler clicks the time.

The tour circles back to the gift shop, where there is pilgrim trash for sale: dashboard saints and glow-in-the-darks; miniature crates of California bubble-gum oranges; mission place mats; moccasins (Sioux).

At the counter, the old lady has been relieved by two pretty teenagers in chiquita blouses who are, like, talking about their boyfriends.

■ ■ ■

In the Archivo General de Indias in Seville are the names and descriptions of missionaries who left their beds and their centuries for the New World. Father Junípero Serra, lector of theology, native of Petra in the province of Majorca, is described by an anonymous sensibility as "of medium height, swarthy, with dark eyes and scant beard."

Father Serra's petition for missionary work should reasonably have languished on a reserve list of older and unlikely candidates. Serra was middle-aged, an academician. Nevertheless, Serra's petition was preferred over those of younger men. In 1749, Father Serra set sail.

This summer, the summer of 1987, Pope John Paul II is coming to California. The expectation on the nightly news and in the morning papers is that the pope, during his visit, will beatify Father Junípero Serra; will recommend Serra to the faithful as a model for actual imitation, which is to rescue Serra from history, to restore him to the present.

I think the Vatican only intends to convey that in her book California is good soil—in the manner of the parable—and, indeed, the fields of California seem especially plenteous of mustard this summer.

California does not look to Rome for justification. California is the Vatican's adversary in a competition for the imagination of the world. Hollywood manufactures 80 percent of the world's supernatural.

Nevertheless, there is considerable media interest in the rumor of beatification. A historical debate is resurrected on the nightly news and in the morning papers. Descendants of Mission Indians hasten to portray Father Serra as an eighteenth-century type of Reverend Moon. The debate swings for balance onto the faces of Franciscan priests who defend the memory of Father Serra. I think the camera is only looking for a way to fill its insidiously bland eye.

Lieutenant Colonel Oliver North is testifying before a congressional committee this summer concerning the fragility of memory, the destruction of evidence.

And a question does linger about the missions. The question hinges upon consent—the question of a democratic age. Were the Mission Indians consensual Christians?

I have decided—apart, but not entirely apart, from shifting documentary evidence concerning the life of Father Serra—to visit the twenty-one missions of California.

■　■　■

Twenty years ago, when Joseph Alioto was the mayor of San Francisco, Mrs. Alioto disappeared. A manhunt ensued, on the nightly news and in the morning papers. Was she abducted? Amnesiac? Has anyone seen this dame?

Within a few days the mayor's wife reappeared, bundled in a mink coat past the paparazzi of her day.

Where had she been? She had been on pilgrimage, she said. She had taken a tour of the California missions in a hired limousine. She draped the black mantilla over her forehead. She pulled the collar of her mink a little more closely about her ears. She wore dark glasses. She paid only in cash.

She said it was something she had always meant to do.

■ ■ ■

Wallet, keys, address book, credit cards . . .

Rumors from a New World—of oceans, monsters, savages—must have excited awe in Serra. I marvel at the piety that could resolve such awe.

Now I can only imagine dread within those dark eyes, though it seems to me as a boy I understood Serra well enough. Our fourth-grade imaginations were bound up in the lives of the saints.

Father Serra was not a saint. Father Serra was a dead pioneer prescribed for our curriculum by the state Board of Education.

Junípero Serra founded twenty-one missions in California—a rosary—stretching from San Diego to Sonoma, each a day's walk from the next—Sister Colette was wrong about that detail—and, as he walked, Serra strewed wild mustard seed about the hillsides.

I imagined a tall man of wide stride and huge strength. In California's fourth-grade mythology, Serra is the tireless traveler, staff in hand.

Father Serra is an authentic pun in California—the Father of the state—civilizer, tamer of savages, planter of shade.

In fact, the staff was a cane. Serra's left foot was infected and it pained him to walk by the time he arrived in California—so much pain that his travel here was on mule or by ship. "In his lifetime, Serra covered a greater distance than did Marco Polo"—Sister Colette knew how to pitch to the fourth-grade imagination.

One foot and then the other foot. The concussion of the foot upon the earth. Serra's journey festering, then leaking through its bindings and into the desert.

"Serra died at sunset on the feast of St. Augustine, in the arms of his beloved Indians."

After all the tears, the farewells, the rolling ocean, the home-sick years, and at the golden apogee of an Indian summer, Sister Mary Colette stood before a fourth-grade class in Sacramento, California. I would take it for granted that a woman with an Irish accent should be my teacher; that I was her child. Had I known of the many travails she had endured to come to me, I would have assumed I was worth it.

■ ■ ■

At Santa Barbara—"the Queen of the Missions"—I ask to see the archives. The director of the archives library is an old Fran-ciscan friar. He takes my hand, but he is not friendly, because all summer journalists have come here to ask questions about Father Serra, and because the archivist has been misquoted.

"I do not like journalists. You should know that. You come here and you want me to make history easy for you."

He points to a shelf behind me.

"Look at those books."

I look.

"They were all written about Father Serra's life. Do you expect me to tell you what is inside?"

Journalists! "You come here from Los Angeles for thirty min-utes; you want to know everything about the past. If you really want to know, then study."

I have not come to ask about Serra. I have come to look at these archives, I flatter. How extraordinary your job is. You are the guardian of California's memory of itself.

But the old man turns away from my voice. What do I want from him? What is there for him to tell me about his work or his life?

He was ordered by his superior to come here, to Santa Barbara, to work in the archives. He rehearses the names of those who preceded him. He is merely carrying on the line.

What else do I want to know?

He was born in Italy, in a house older than any of these California missions. What is two hundred years?

There is nothing interested in his voice. "Every important state document, dating from before the American takeover in 1848, everything pertaining to California before that time, is here—not in Sacramento."

He looks at his watch. He has to be at the bank by three o'clock.

"Let me give you a tour . . ." (to get me moving). "Letters here . . . baptismal records" (on computer sheets)—Indians baptized at all of the California missions. Deaths. First communions. Marriages.

Back to the bookshelves.

"These belonged to the missionaries; the books they brought with them from Spain and from Mexico."

Then these are the seeds of Europe. I reach to touch one of the bindings.

But the old man's hand is at my elbow.

"I'm sorry there isn't more time, Mr. Rodriguez."

■ ■ ■

Elizabeth Blake is considering paint in a jar, chalky, watery, brown. Elizabeth Blake is an anthropologist, an artist, a Catholic; she says her work is a form of devotion. She is spending this year at Mission San Luis Rey, restoring decorations on the walls of the church. On a Tuesday morning I find her painting the lower portion of a wall where generations of children have run their fingers.

Elizabeth Blake tells me the best time for her is early morning, when the main doors of the church are locked and she can hear the sprinklers outside. "There is a special aura in old places of worship."

By and by, the tourists come to watch her paint. And, as they watch, questions form in their minds about history, like:

Which is the Indian part?

She cannot say.

The missions do not belong to any one culture, she tells them. "Look at that dome. There's nothing like it in any other California mission. The dome is not Spanish, but Arabic in design."

An Arabic dome on a Spanish church named to the honor of a French king who launched a crusade against the infidel: medieval Spain was just such an arabesque of ironies. For centuries, Christian Spain brooded upon the expulsion of foreigners—the rule of the Moor, the heterodoxy of the Jew. Christian Spain realized its obsession in the fifteenth century; cut off the Arab's head; sent the Jew packing. By the late fifteenth century, however, Spain had changed its complexion, turned a corridor of thought. Protracted preoccupation with the foreigner left the Spaniard, alone among Europeans, an internationalist (the Jewish heritage, after all). And from Spain's long association with the Arab, Spanish Christians took an Islamic notion of spiritual kinship—religious fraternity as binding as blood. The same year that Spain purged the foreign from itself, Spain set sail to convert the world.

Three hundred years later—the breadth of an ocean, the height of a tree—a Spanish priest in California instructed an Indian, whether in harsh or in yielding tones we know not, to paint decorations on the wall of a mission church unmistakably Moorish in design.

Five hundred years later, I get lost looking for Mission San Gabriel, so I arrive late and have to talk a priest into letting me into the darkening church "for a look." The priest may well be suspicious, but he waits graciously as I look at the ceiling, at the altar. "Wonderful light," I whisper.

"There," he says, leading me out, "you've seen it."

I have not seen it.

The point of the missions was their linkage, each to each. California was the northernmost extension of a mission system that connected Mexico with Europe, with Spain, with Rome. The landscape of California was continuous with the landscape of Mexico. The sky a dome over all.

Spain worried about Russian settlements along the northern coast of California. Spain intended to bring the California Indians firmly within its leathery embrace. The Spanish missions would convey the Indians from a nomadic, to an agrarian, to a Spanish way of life.

Whereas the Puritans in New England regarded the Indians from a distance as inimical to their purpose, Spanish priests made a beeline for Indians. Indians were the reason they had come.

The postmodern imagination of California Indians is of a surfer nation, trusting and entrusted to nature.

The postmodern judgment of Serra derives from our imagination of Indians as innocent. Serra did not approach naked Indians with the reverence we might feel for the angelic dolphins, twirling within their cubes of salty sky.

Rome had decreed that Indians had souls, were therefore the spiritual equals of Europeans—equal, too, in their need for evangelization. Serra could not, therefore, have seen the Indians as innocents.

Serra cannot, then, have stepped onto paradise.

For history and Eden are irreconcilable ideas. The lessons of Genesis would have consoled Serra that history is inevitable, tragedy inevitable, innocence impossible. Serra's California was an impure idea, a postlapsarian, Christian idea. Serra described California with the poignance of postlapsarian irony:

> *Then I saw what I could hardly begin to believe when I read about it . . . namely that they go about entirely naked like Adam in paradise before the Fall. . . .*

The Father of California did not discover California. Father Serra did not divine the sites for what would later become California's principal cities and towns. He traveled to where Indians had already logically established themselves, within benevolent climates, near fresh water, and he proceeded to lure Indians to his purpose, which was convenient to the king's purpose.

Serra called the Indian beloved. Sister Colette was right about that.

By the waters of baptism, Indians were made to bear the weight of the raising of the missions. Did priests convert the Indians by breaking their backs?

A story survives of Serra preaching to the Indians, preaching of a merciful God, even as he beat upon his chest with a rock. Defenders of Father Serra speak of "historical context."

As I pace this tamped and watered cloister, I begin to wonder what a garden could have meant to the Indians who first planted one. Would the notion of nature enclosed have seemed a sacrilege or would it have seemed the beginning of some interesting new order?

Father Serra has traditionally been credited by the California textbook industry with having taught Indians to become "self-reliant." The European version of self-reliance for the Indian meant pitting the Indian against nature.

The Spaniard had come to overturn nature—that was the

point—had come to tear the tree out of the sky, kill the bird, strip the branches, build the freeway—in the sense that nature (by authority of Genesis) was man's tool and not sacrosanct.

The Spaniard had come to civilize. How, then, should the Indian survive unless the Indian become reconciled to civilization?

Father Serra can play two parts in the tragedy of California. If he is the first Lost Man, the perceiving Adam, he is as well the Angel of the Fiery Sword, forbidding Eden.

For postmodern Californians the mission garden can only seem a pastoral regression. And, insofar as we hate what California has become—its distance from metaphors of paradise—we must blame Serra, the Father of California.

■　■　■

Since the Protestant arrival here, California has worn metaphors appropriate to paradise. When you are in gridlock on the San Diego Freeway, it is difficult to believe yourself the denizen of an earthly paradise. Only if climate is the criterion (and it may be)—neither the bluest sky nor the greenest tree, but we are temperate withal.

On Interstate 15, heading north, three lanes narrow to a single lane of passage. An officer of the U.S. Border Patrol holds his hand up to stop me. He peers through the windshield to study my face. His car radio issues incomplete commands. He is looking for "illegals." I am driving a rented car. He waves me on.

On my car radio, a Native American woman accuses Father Serra of "cultural genocide."

I imagine Elizabeth Blake alone in her cavernous church, retracing the Catholic narrative line. I watch as she introduces brown into a channel between two black lines.

Before I left, Elizabeth Blake told me a Mexican man who had done some work in the Arabic dome left his initials up there. I asked her if she felt any like temptation to memorialize herself. She smiled then, as she spooned more of the pigment into a coffee jar.

"Nope. I've made my offering. I want to remain as much an anonymity as the Indian who first painted this wall."

■ ■ ■

When Mexico won independence from Spain, California became Mexican territory. Within ten years, Mexico decreed the "secularization" of the California missions, giving the mission churches over to diocesan clergy. Mission landholdings would henceforward be administered by Mexican governors.

The government of Mexico envisioned an eventual return of mission lands to Indians. But soon Mexico needed to raise money against an anticipated invasion by the United States. By 1844, every mission but Santa Barbara had been sold. Indians abandoned the missions. The churches and cloisters fell to ruin.

Summers came and winters—wheels of weather.

The Indian year taught the rule of nature, a cycle of seasons, of weather and provender; a migratory path through the stars that ended where it began.

And rain pelted the mud walls of the missions.

The Spanish year was likewise repetitive, likewise didactic. The liturgical year was a synchronous wheel-casing superimposed upon nature, moving as nature moves; a mythological hubcap of two major solstices—the Incarnation of God and the Redemption of Man. The Spanish weather Christianized nature.

And birds nestled in the eaves of the sanctuary.

And grass sprang up from the broken flagstones.

By and by, the Americans came.

The Puritan year was a wheel as a canister of film is a wheel —making the future by unmaking the past. The Puritan year measured Pilgrim's progress, measured only distance; the past would never overtake the future.

On fine days in early spring, when the sky was rinsed and the hills were green, these ruins beckoned Americans as places for picnics and Sunday painters.

Lovers carved their initials on the olive trees in the cloister, and children dug for rusty spikes.

And the old walls collapsed.

Part Two: Daughter of the Golden West

In 1883, Helen Hunt Jackson traveled overland to California. A type of the intrepid, indispensable Jamesian observer, Mrs. Jackson was a New England Yankee, an abolitionist, an anti-papist. She poked among the ruins. She listened to some old stories. Then she settled herself down to write *Ramona*, a deathless romance of Spanish California.

Ramona has survived less in its intended kinship with *Uncle Tom's Cabin* than as a ranchero *Gone With the Wind*. Helen Hunt Jackson meant to document the mistreatment of California Indians. Instead, she ignited a passion in the bosoms of Protestants for guitars and roses and raven-haired lovers.

Carey McWilliams, an historian who came to California forty years after Mrs. Jackson, wrote unambiguously about the mistreatment of Mexicans in California, but he was rueful regarding a latter-day Protestant reconciliation with the Spanish past. McWilliams found it incredible that Americans in the 1880s should have undertaken to restore the missions, and that the interest in the missions (those "picturesque charnel houses") was so much greater in the more Protestant southern half of the state than in northern California.

McWilliams mocked three emblems of what he termed the

synthetic past: "the Franciscan padre praying at sundown in the Mission garden, lovely Ramona and brave Alessandro fleeing through the foothills of Mt. Jacinto, and the Old Don sunning himself in the courtyard of his rancho."

Californians who dressed up in dingle-hats and mantillas to celebrate the Days of the Dons were the same Californians, McWilliams wrote, who would not otherwise have had anything to do with the Hispanic remnant of California—Californians who would never have ventured into the Mexican sides of towns. All such fandango really celebrated, according to McWilliams, was California's "fantasy heritage."

Thinking about McWilliams, I begin to wonder about the quality of my own nostalgia. A radio station in Santa Cruz is playing twenty-two Oldies but Goodies. My nostalgia for Oldies is not a pining after sexual experience that was truly mine so much as it is a yearning for a time—and the music I heard only incidentally—when I fancied myself to have cut loose from the past. Prom music should remind me of how separate I felt during those years of my growing up, but it doesn't. It doesn't remind me of myself at all. It reminds me of freeways being built in California; it reminds me of my faith in the future. My nostalgia is for a time when I felt myself free of nostalgia.

In *Ramona* there is a scene in which the proud señora of the rancho, really the villainess of the piece, defiantly plants crosses on the landscape against the advent of the gringos, who will see them and be forced to remember that the Catholic faith—a Spanish world—had preceded them and would forever haunt their optimism.

Two theologies vied for primacy in California; two theologies met here. The northward, the communal, the Catholic impulse dragged the gargantuan trap of European civilization in its wake, extending the Great World. The Protestant, the westward, the individual impulse favored amnesia; left all behind. The Protestant myth of California was constructed by people who came from the East. Vestiges of Spanish colonial served to remind Protestants that they were no longer part of the East. The adoption of Spanish customs was a way for newcomers to celebrate their distance from their own pasts.

I begin to notice the collision of cultures played out in every dry creek I cross and on every freeway exit sign. Anglo names suggest the force of pioneer personalities—Irvine, Newman, King City—fading contracts in strongboxes. Or else the names are plain and descriptive of the way the land looked—Pleasant Hill, Riverbank. Most of the Spanish names are holy names.

The central mystery of Roman Catholicism is the mystery of the Incarnation. God became man. The Word took on flesh.

Time itself was incarnate. Time was measured by a sacred liturgical calendar (we still count time as distance from the event of the Incarnation). Safe arrivals did not occur on Tuesdays or on Fridays, but upon the feast days of saints. Place names became sacred names. Thus the map of California mirrors the map of heaven. Thus California becomes a Star Map of the celestial Beverly Hills.

Though the bells of the missions are now as muffled as the stuffed mouths of corpses, living Californians—such was the genius of Spain—must yet compose a litany of sorts to get from one end of town to the other: "Take the San Bernardino to the San Gabriel turnoff," for example.

In the years following the Mexican-American War, pragmatic Americans never thought to change the Spanish names on the map, though Americans seem to have agreed among themselves to mispronounce all Spanish names. And Americans have their leveling ways: La Ciudad de Nuestra Señora la Reina de los Angeles de Porciuncula has become, in one hundred years, L. A.

■ ■ ■

In San Francisco I visit the headquarters of the Native Daughters of the Golden West, because I have noticed the society thanked so often and so prominently on mission plaques and in mission pamphlets.

The society's executive secretary speaks to me briefly of "venerating" the past and of "revering" the values of California's pioneers. The secretary excuses herself for a moment to answer a telephone call.

A breeze lifts the curtain of an open window. From some other part of the building come bright, crystalline bars, and then the low, bumblebee bars of a piano being played, some old air. There is a slight acrid scent to the room, a scent associated with remembrance. An astringent polish on the furniture or on the floors, perhaps.

The Native Daughter of the Golden West puts down the telephone receiver and, in answer to a question I had previously asked, she tells me the organization has more Protestant members than Catholic. She herself is a Catholic, though she is quick with a disclaimer: her interest in the missions is purely historical. "I would be as interested in helping to preserve a log cabin."

The Native Daughters of the Golden West is a nondenominational, nonethnic organization of women that honors the achievements of the men and women who built California. Members must be native-born Californians—an odd requirement insofar as the men and women who built California were born elsewhere.

The first "parlor" of Native Daughters was convened in Jackson in the 1880s. Jackson was a nineteenth-century gold town. Original Daughters must have been the daughters of parents who came to California looking for gold.

The Missions

The Daughter of the Golden West had seen her father, her mama, her uncle Cecil—that scamp—grow old and die, and all their witty sayings and all their strong advice. Her inheritance was California.

What the sorrowing Daughter could not abide was the leveling shrug of a state that honors only the future. Such a state condemned her parents to oblivion.

So the Native Daughter started saving things. She put her father's gold watch under a bell jar on the mantelpiece. Then she started to rope off places and call them historic because the past had once happened there. In the course of her project, the Daughter must end up violating the values of her parents—themselves restless, westering—in favor of her own rootedness.

The missions were a rubble of popish nonsense, but they were the oldest things around. It was not sentimentality that recalled the missions; it was not faith. It was fear of oblivion. If the missions were allowed to sink back into the earth, then what hope for the enduring influence of any Californian? Why live here at all?

■ ■ ■

I enter the "oldest building in California"—a small chapel at San Juan Capistrano where Junípero Serra celebrated mass. I kneel to say a prayer for Nancy—a prayer that should plead like a scalpel. A camera flashes at the rear of the church. Distracted, I fall to formula. *Pray for us now and at the hour of our death.* A group of tourists has entered the sanctuary to examine the crucifix, one of them laughs. I cross myself ostentatiously, I genuflect, I leave the chapel for the sun-drenched cloister.

Where I ask the docents at San Juan Capistrano why the tourists come.

They come to feed the birds.

They come to see the gardens.

They come for the history.

They come for the history, all agree.

The Australian students tell me they saw the historical marker along the freeway and thought they might as well take a look. They'd been driving a long time. They are not Catholics. How far is Disneyland?

A woman leading several children says she is here for the "history lesson," also for the restrooms.

Now that the missions no longer exert an active presence in the life of California, they nevertheless continue as a passive, a quaint, a subversive influence. Tourists come in spite of the religious aspect of the missions. Indeed, the missions are picturesque; they are romantic; they lure the Californian off the freeway for being so different—seeming so pristine—amidst the ancient ruins of twentieth-century California. And perhaps, as we approach the twenty-first century, we look for nothing so much as a reason to get off the freeway.

Perhaps, too, the more we forget, the less we comprehend, the more easily we see what the Indians first saw.

"Mama, what's thi-i-i-s-s-s-s?" asks a little girl who is ringing a rosy around the pedestal of a baptismal font.

"That's where the Indians cooked their food," answers Mama.

■ ■ ■

Everyone told me I would like La Purísima best. You really feel what it must have been like, people said.

The state of California acquired the property in the 1930s. Visitors find La Purísima alone on its landscape, a few miles from Lompoc. The parking lot is hidden by thickets of scrub and at a field's distance from the mission compound. Yes, you can imagine the solitude of the landscape; you can imagine the hardness of the life. Perhaps I was expecting too much. La Purísima reminds me of nothing so much as those churches the Soviet government used to ridicule by making of them shrines to history. La Purísima is Williamsburg and Sutter's Fort and worse. The state's insistence that here are matters only of fact is depressing, the triumph of history over memory.

I like the gardens—real, life-sustaining gardens. There are swallows and red ants and the sound of the wind in an ancient tree. A Spanish-speaking family is making an interested tour of the mission gardens. Young fingers tear herbaceous leaves, then hold them up for Grandmother to test with the force of her bony jaw, to tell them what.

These rooms are cold. They aren't the rooms anything happened in, except perhaps the squabbles of decorators employed by the state of California to arrange typical or authentic artifacts in such a way as to suggest that the community living here has been forewarned of our arrival, has made the beds, dropped the waffle iron—or whatever that thing is—and walked over the hill, out of sight. The church is no longer a church, that is the worst of it. No sanctuary lamp burns at La Purísima. In the chapel there is a recorded, authentic chant, looping over and over again.

That Catholic faith may survive in the missions, or in spite of the missions, is no longer the point of them. Protestants, venerating history, rebuilt second-class relics of the Church; rebuilt their antithesis; regilded the high altar of Europe. And they did so in the spirit of the Mission Indians, uncomprehending.

Native Sons and Daughters—preservation societies—have so diligently divorced place or artifact from intention that they become handmaidens of amnesia. A secular altar guild that will not distinguish between a flatiron and a chalice, between a log cabin and a mission church, preserves only strangeness.

But their impulse to preserve was already admitting the Spanish side. The notion that the past implicates the future and that we are not alone on the landscape—these ideas were planted in California by Franciscans.

In the 1950s, the Native Daughters of the Golden West helped rebuild tiny Soledad Mission in the Salinas Valley. Members of the society met with interested townspeople at a local Methodist church to organize the restoration. Today, Soledad Mission is maintained by a civic committee; mass is celebrated here only occasionally.

The tragic effigy of Nuestra Señora de la Soledad stands over the altar, dressed in the weeds of a Spanish widow. Bereft, uncompensated, a prisoner of time in her arid little chapel—she is Europe, the Catholic queen. She is Eleanor of Aquitaine. Mary Queen of Scots. Can it be any coincidence, I ask myself, that Soledad State Prison, a few miles away, was built within the patronage of this tragic queen?

■ ■ ■

San Antonio de Pala is not one of the twenty-one missions; it is a "sub-mission," the only one surviving, founded in 1815 by the Franciscans, about thirty miles inland from San Luis Rey. San Antonio still serves an Indian congregation.

There is a gift shop. I am the only tourist. A couple of kids are playing in the schoolyard. A dog sprawls upon the threshold of the church.

The chapel is dark. Here the scent of missions is redoubled, a smell of the absence of light, a cellar smell. An antique gas heater near the entrance seems as much a relic of olden times on this hot day as the painted reredos behind the altar.

The gardens at Pala seem continuous with the nineteenth century. They are not restored; they are simply tended. Someone has planted a cactus in a ceramic Dutch shoe. Over by the parking lot a small marquee records how, in 1903, after a newly arrived priest whitewashed the interior walls of the chapel, the Pala

Indians, rather in the spirit of the Daughters of the Golden West, defiantly repainted the wall decorations from memory.

■   ■   ■

Sonoma Mission is a museum. But the ruin of a Spanish idea seems now to anticipate some future California. The countryside surrounding the mission is rearranging itself according to Umbrian models of the picturesque. On the town square, Main Street façades of Protestant decades are being refurbished in Mediterranean styles. The grain-and-feed store has become a trattoria. A few miles from the town is a resort-spa called Sonoma Mission Inn. City people come here for retreats. Health has replaced holiness as a goal. Sonoma Mission Inn is a cloister for voluptuaries. Yet everywhere about these hillsides one senses the shadow of a mission, the rehearsal of a mission way of life or, at any rate, an attempt to discover what a phrase like that might mean.

Is it possible California is Catholic, as New England is Protestant, by virtue of its mnemonic ruins?

Betty at the gift shop at Mission San Antonio tells me even non-Catholics usually buy something for their Catholic friends back home—"just to be taking something away with them." They come for an hour. They drop coins in the fountain, just to be leaving something behind. An old man sitting with his wife in the shade of a pepper tree tells me they have come here every year to have their picture taken. People come because memory is here. People write their names in the guest book by the door and they are remembered.

In a side chapel of Santa Barbara Mission, there is an open visitors' book. "Pray for my family," wrote one stranger's hand. Beneath, in childish capitals, PLEASE PRAY FOR ME AND MY BROTHER.

At Soledad, the lady who works in the gift shop sits out by the

Coke machine on the patio, fanning herself with a fly swatter. She points out the pink rose bush she herself planted on the west side of the mission. She is not Catholic (Baptist, she confides). She and her husband live out back in a trailer.

She is keeping her eye on a cheerful party of archaeology students from UCLA over by the parking lot. I watch the students dusting with big brushes the broken shapes they hold between thumb and middle finger. Wasps malevolently preen themselves upon the watery surfaces of sluicing trays. Rock music rises from a portable radio.

"They're wasting their time, though," the gift-shop lady says. "There's no more past out there to discover."

■ ■ ■

I've never met Angelina Alioto. I don't even know what she looks like. I imagine Regine Crespin (the Marschallin), or Morgana King. Tonight, in my motel room—the El Padre—I imagine myself the mayor's unhappy wife. I have taken a bath. I've turned the lamps on and off. I've looked through the empty drawers. I've watched a half hour of *Jeopardy* on TV.

On *Jeopardy* the question is the answer. For example:

GOD GAVE THIS TO MOSES ON MT. SINAI.

The contestant is a college student. She ventures a guess.

"What is . . . a boat?"

The rude buzzer. Not a boat, dummy. A boat?

Followed by the news: The pope. The pope is still coming to California. A coven of clown-painted transvestites dances in a circle. They are dressed as nuns, mocking heroic lives. Surely the Knights of Columbus of my childhood—old men with sabers and plumed hats and half-capes—surely such knights would have done battle with these impious witches. But the Knights of Certainty are all dead. This is a new age.

Have I, like the California Indians, sought some refuge from a world that can no longer make much sense of me? Have I, like the mayor's wife, sought to preserve my faith within a wisteriad cloister—sought some Sonoma Mission Inn of the soul?

Here, in the El Padre Motel, my nostalgia seems complete. The missions were not meant to last, that is the lesson. "Let them fall, let them sink, let them not be remembered. . . ." I imagine the voice of Father Serra.

The missions the Franciscans built were not built for us, for the mayor's wife or me. The missions the Protestants reconstructed were not reconstructed for us. We are Catholics. We must look for our faith in the California that was created from the missions.

I have seen all I want to see of the missions. My interest is purely historical. Just something I had always meant to do.

∎ ∎ ∎

Summer's end.

Vouchers, receipts, notepads, brochures . . .

Oliver North has become a national hero. The Vatican, governed by latent discretion, has decided to postpone the beatification of Father Serra until after the pope's visit.

Junípero Serra lies buried beneath a wreath of black myrtle at Mission Carmel; sleeps through a secular age.

The beloved Indians of Sister Colette's lesson—Marías and Diegos—lie in unmarked graves, revised fictional plots, bordered with abalone shells.

Franciscan memory oxidizes upon a shelf—books, painstaking journals, hagiographies, all bound up with the sordid skins of animals.

Nearly all of the missions have been restored, repainted, rewatered into versions of paradise, the interior castles of Spanish mysticism or the Moorish gardens of Allah.

There is a plaque on the north side of the state capitol in Sacramento, honoring the Sisters of Mercy. I discovered the plaque by accident, killing time waiting for an appointment. I had the impression then—new to me—that I had known pioneer women as a boy.

When I last saw Sister Colette, I was middle-aged, she was near death. She was at the Mercy mother house near Auburn. A white turban swaddled her tender skull. She had waited at her bedroom window all afternoon to see my car approach. We sat in a parlor and had tea. I told her I had been reading about the Sisters of Mercy—how remarkable they seem to me now! Could she tell me something more about the dauntless heiress Mother Baptist Russell, leading her company of women all that way from Ireland in the nineteenth century?

Sister Colette was distracted by fatigue and by pain.

"Well," she said after a pause, "when those young nuns traveled across Central America, they were carried on the backs of black natives through the jungle.

"Can't you just see them, Richard, bouncing along on the backs of those men and squawking like parrots?"

Her shoulders rose and fell like little wings, simulating merriment.

Part Three: Savage

San José is the most recently restored of the missions, completed in 1985, rebuilt from the ground up—a complete fake. And, for that, probably the nearest approach to the past.

It was the custom for missionaries in Latin America to paint their churches white to dazzle Indians; lure Indians down from the hills. Mission San José similarly dazzles, lures.

New suburbs, bedroom communities, are closing in on Mission San José—completing the missions, I now believe Father Serra would have said. Yellow bulldozers are skinning the parched hide

off the back of California. The developers give their new subdivisions Spanish names. One such development of new "Heritage
Estates" has streets with names like Paseo Padre Parkway. A tiny
nineteenth-century cemetery spilling off the side of a hill poses
the lone reminder of a pastoral California that will be lost in this
generation.

A teenage boy wanders down the center aisle of the church at
Mission San José, carrying a skateboard. He is naked to his waist.

Inside the museum, photographs document the stages of re-
construction (1983–85), with special thanks to Coors Distributing
Company of Hayward; the Union Oil Foundation; the Gleason
family; Dan Carter of the Portman Company (for carving the choir
loft); Carlos Rohales of Northwest Masonry.

Throughout, accuracy has been scientifically achieved; imper-
fections of Indian construction have been "faithfully" reproduced.

A plexiglass window in the museum wall bids us examine an
exposition of original adobe. Adobe is gray. Adobe is dehydrated
mud. It is clod. Stuck in its mass are wisps of straw, bits of gravel
and shell, collapsed cobweb. Adobe is mud shaped by human
intention.

Mix the mud, the shells, the sand, the straw with living water.
Shovel some dung from the cart. Mule dung. Priest dung. Indian
dung.

This dung is made to cleave to the sky. Daub it on the sky
and it will stick like a swallow's dome: SERRAMONTE SHOPPING
CENTER. MICCION NISSAN. MISSION DRIVE-IN. TACO BELL. JUNIPERO
SERRA FREEWAY. MISSION BAPTIST CHURCH. SERRA TAXI COMPANY.
MISSION WEDDING CHAPEL (WEDDINGS ANYTIME/ANYPLACE).

Father Serra did not have the strength of resolve to face his
aged parents, to tell them of his departure for the missions.
Instead, Serra composed a letter which he entreated a relative to
read to his parents after the boat had sailed.

Goodbye, my dear father! Farewell, dear mother of mine . . .
Goodbye and farewell!

A boy wanders down the center aisle, naked to his waist, his thongs slap, slap, slapping upon the tiles of the mission floor. He pushes his sunglasses up to rest on the crown of his head.

He pauses with savage innocence and a certain grace.

CHAPTER SIX

The Head of
Joaquín Murrieta

This is a story about a human head in a jar. This is a story about stories, about Joaquín Murrieta, a nineteenth-century Mexican, a matinee idol among bandits, who may or may not have been a murderer, who may or may not have been killed and beheaded one yellow morning in Fresno County in 1853. This is a story about legends and lies and the romantic stories Californians have told one another and withheld from impressionable children for over one hundred years.

The story begins with a letter sent to Governor George Deukmejian by a Jesuit priest named Alberto Huerta. Copies were mailed to well-known Hispanics. César Chávez got one; so did Octavio Paz and Henry Cisneros. In his letter, Father Huerta asks the governor's help in finding the severed head of Joaquín Murrieta—"the symbol of an unglorious past"—so that the past and the head might be buried as one beneath several hundred pounds of the alkaline dirt we call California.

Who knows if anyone in the governor's office had ever heard of Joaquín Murrieta. And who knows if Governor Deukmejian

133

saw the letter. For a reply, Father Huerta received abashed greetings from a polite assistant. The governor is grateful. The governor asked me to respond. Sorry to say the governor is in no position. Cordially yours.

■ ■ ■

The story is best told by a grandmother. Children are sitting on the steps of the back porch, sipping Kool-Aid, shooing flies. Tell us a story.

The Sierra Madre is full of caves. And the caves are full of secrets.... Shh ... shhh ... Listen. Once upon a time, a Mexican came to California from Sonora, the land of white deserts and big blue mountains. His name was Joaquín. They used to tell us be good or Joaquín Murrieta will write your name down in his cave. Then he will come one day when you are all alone and pull you up on his horse and ride away. And the boys wanted him to. And the girls, some of them wanted him to. He was young and very handsome, with dark eyes ... like yours.

He walked to California with his beautiful wife, all that way from Mexico, sleeping outside under the stars. Murrieta and his beautiful wife came up after the gringos had stolen California from us. So they were not welcome around here. They worked the land for a while; they grew some corn. They heard some miners were getting rich in the hills. So Joaquín talked it over with his brother and they decided they'd try to find some gold for themselves. They traveled up to the foothills and made camp by the river. Then, one night when the moon was high, high, some gringos got drunk and they came over to Joaquín's camp. They tied Joaquín up and whipped him like he was a horse. Then they took his wife and they did bad things to her. Right in front of Joaquín's eyes, they hanged his brother. Joaquín swore revenge under the moon of that same night. They say he followed every one of those gringos and he killed them, one by one.

The Head of Joaquín Murrieta

Yes, he became a robber, but not a bad man maybe. He gave what he stole to poor people. He stole horses, beautiful horses. He was like the wind stealing clouds. He kept the blackest horse for himself. They said his heart was as black as his chin. He wore a black hat with a black feather and a big black cape. And you could only see his eyes.

The gringos were afraid of him; they were always looking over their shoulders. For he spoke many disguises. They say he could talk like a gringo. They say he could talk Chinese. Sometimes he pretended he was a little old man. Sometimes he pretended he was a girl with golden curls and a little high voice.

If Joaquín was a bad man, those gringos made him bad. They tried and they tried to get him, but he always disappeared. He had tunnels all over California like a jackrabbit. They would think they had found his hiding place and they would set fire to his cabin, but he was already on the other side of the hill, laughing at them. Then one day they caught him out in the sun, in a yellow field full of gopher holes and rattlesnake holes, and Joaquín couldn't tell which was a gopher hole and which was a rattlesnake hole and which was his escape tunnel. They shot him—pop—they cut off his head and they put it in a jar like a big angry pepper so they could laugh at him forever.

But then, they say, Joaquín went after the gringos who had killed him, one by one.

■ ■ ■

I first saw the name of Alberto Huerta as the byline on an essay in Spanish he had written about "Joaquín Murrieta and the Odyssey of Hispanic California Writers." (I was the sad example.) Several months later I received a curious c.c. in my mail—a letter to the governor of California signed by Alberto Huerta, S.J. I decided to give Father Huerta a call.

We first meet in a transient visitors' lounge of the Jesuit residence at the University of San Francisco, where Father Huerta teaches. At his back is a bookshelf without books, a desk without drawers. It is late afternoon on the Fourth of July. Outside the window some Arab students kneel on a carpet of lawn, facing east.

Father Huerta is short, balding, early in his forties. He insists on calling me *Ree-car-do*, baroquely sounding each syllable. We like each other from the start. For the holiday he is wearing a striped tie, red, white, and blue, against a brick-red shirt.

Father Huerta is not joking by the time he raises the head of Joaquín Murrieta. "Legend has it that Murrieta was killed and beheaded, his head brought back by state troopers for reward money. No one knows exactly what happened to that head. But if there is a head in a jar still around, that head should be buried. Buried for humanitarian reasons (we're talking about a human being!), and buried because the head symbolizes the struggle and the suffering of the Mexican people in California. What the governor seems not to grasp is the state's obligation in this business. Since the state paid more than five thousand dollars to gun Joaquín Murrieta down, the least it can do is bring him to rest."

Father Huerta imagines a solemn funeral mass, perhaps at Mission Santa Clara—a service to which all Californians could come. "All of us need to face our guilts and fears, if we are to become reconciled to one another." A funeral, but a fiesta too. He imagines Joan Baez composing *corridos* for the occasion. (She got a letter.)

■ ■ ■

In California today there are many places named for Joaquín Murrieta. There are springs and spas and trails, two towns. There are rock formations and caves and ridges, valleys, creeks, post offices, and Mexican restaurants. There is a slough. There are probably children. But ask around. Joaquín Murrieta? Some hazard a guess.

There are other, older Californians who remember. His life may be one of the state's most repeated tales, a story like the story of the Donner party or the story of Marilyn Monroe.

Murrieta long ago assumed international fame as the hero of pulp novels and melodramas. Joaquín's life is sung in Mexican *corridos*. His life is told in French. His exploits were known in Madrid. Chile's pre-eminent poet, Pablo Neruda, made him a countryman and gave him a play—*Fulgor y Muerte de Joaquín Murieta, Bandido Chileño*.

Joaquín Murrieta (the surname has ten variant spellings) comes up from Mexico with a brother; he comes up with a half-brother; he comes with a brother-in-law. He is unmarried. He is married. His wife is named Rosita or she is Carmela. She is Rosita-Carmela. Rosita-Carmela becomes Mariana Higuera. Mariana Higuera is descended from Aztec royalty. . . .

The most influential account of the life in English was written by John Rollin Ridge. Published in 1854, only one year after Joaquín Murrieta was supposed to have died, this highly colored "life" inspired the romantic embellishments of subsequent biographies. Indeed, the life has become so legendary that most historians have grown skeptical on all counts. Joseph Henry Jackson, for example, concluded that Ridge's "preposterous little book" is merely the trash of dime novels.

Certainly crimes were committed up and down California early in the 1850s, all of which were blamed on the ubiquitous "Joaquín." In response to public outrage, the governor of California empowered a onetime Texas Ranger, Harry Love, to organize a posse. Posters offered a reward for THE BANDIT JOAQUIN. Nobody knew whom to look for.

In 1980, an amateur California historian named Frank F. Latta published a wonderful, exhaustive, unedited, sometimes unreadable book. Latta's *Joaquín Murrieta and His Horse Gangs* is an epic of California. There are photographs of every site connected with Joaquín's sojourn here. Many of these feature squinting Latta children in the foreground—souvenirs of Sunday drives with Papa. There are hundreds of interviews with survivors and relatives of survivors from Joaquín's era. Spanish voices. Old Indian voices. English voices. Homesteaders who have lived on into the twentieth century. Californians as old as the state. Their stories strangely cohere.

Joaquín Murrieta existed. There were five men named Joaquín associated with horse gangs, and in one gang there were two men named Joaquín Murrieta. (To distinguish between them, Latta gives the heroic Joaquín the appellation "El Famoso.") Joaquín El Famoso came up from Sonora during the California gold rush. He worked the land. He was later robbed, and his wife was assaulted by a drunken band of Americans. Joaquín El Famoso became a horse thief. He ran with a gang that included the psychopath Manuel Duarte ("Three-Fingered Jack"). The odd thing, the oddest thing, about Latta's book is that it confirms the outline of Joaquín's life in legend.

What remains uncertain is the altruism attributed to the mythic Joaquín. There is evidence to suggest that Mexicans feared Joaquín Murrieta as thoroughly as other Californians feared him. Especially late in his life Murrieta seems to have stolen from anyone unlucky enough to have crossed his path. Maybe the Robin Hood part of the legend has persisted so long among Mexicans because Mexicans felt they had a share in Murrieta's victimization; thus perhaps a share in Murrieta's revenge.

American writers commonly depict a figure of raven sheen and aristocratic demeanor, a California Eros. (A friend who grew up in a small Valley town in the 1950s remembers that the city librarian kept two books from children, unless they had notes of permission from their parents. One was *Lady Chatterley's Lover*; the other was *The Life of Joaquín Murrieta with Illustrations*.)

Joaquín Murrieta becomes blond in some versions, tall, broad-shouldered, green-eyed. But most romances imagine the darker man. In the Rollin Ridge account, Joaquín rides into the town of Stockton one Sunday morning, his black hair gleaming on his shoulders; his eye indifferent to curious stares as the townspeople whisper and wonder where he is from. It is the first act of an operetta.

Joaquín straddles two worlds. The handsome stranger appears in the mining-town saloon. He is perfectly (and without accent) bilingual. He passes among the *norteamericanos* until, like El Cid, he proclaims himself—"It is I, Joaquín!"—and escapes into the night with the gringos' money.

He is a great blade and lover, with waiting women beneath every willow. In Mexican versions, Joaquín's beauty confirms his innocence. In American versions, the red lip, the glittering eye entail the blackest heart. The leveled corpse is made pretty, no longer an object of fear to Americans. And if Joaquín Murrieta were simply a cutthroat Adonis, then nothing much about him would finally matter.

But what if this beauty was not ironic? What if Joaquín was a good man made monstrous? What would that say about the place that transfigured him?

Even as the body of Murrieta lies dissected upon an historian's slab, the myth has passed whole into the hands of poets—to Pablo Neruda, to "Joaquin" Miller, to William Everson, to the anonymous Mexican singers who compose ballads. Listen to the stories, the songs, the poems about the life and you will believe that something terrible and sad happened in California once upon a time.

■ ■ ■

It is nearly three o'clock on a Wednesday at the Balboa Cafe on Fillmore Street. No one seems in any hurry to get back to work. Our waitress intones the bucolic of the day: pasta with goat cheese, smoked duck, pine nuts, and sun-dried tomatoes. Father Huerta orders an omelet—"plain." He seems not to take any notice of the people around us; they probably take as little notice of us.

For months Huerta has been phoning me with "leads," wanting to know how my Murrieta essay progresses. There is no Murrieta essay, I tell him. And there won't be. He sends me books and articles, letters and photocopies. The more energetic he becomes—he seems to be calling me to come to terms with California—the more I pull back. *This* California, the California of Fillmore Street, of blond women and Nautilus-educated advertising executives, this California of pastels and pasta salads is where I live.

It feels like having tea with the hound of heaven. Father Huerta is making a mess. Our table is cluttered with papers and books and flecks of omelet foam. Some letters fall to the floor. Excuse me. Thank you.

Look here. He wants to show me this—a letter he received from Auxiliary Bishop Juan Arzube of Los Angeles. The bishop was apparently troubled by Huerta's appeal to the governor. The bishop sought the advice of some expert—a California historian, it seems. The historian's (anonymous) opinion is attached: "This weird request should be responded to cautiously."

Father Huerta is wounded by the judgment. But surely, I say, you must realize how odd your plan for a Murrieta funeral must seem to some people? How political the gesture will seem?

No. The burial of Joaquín Murrieta is not political. No one is winning or losing. What is at stake is a symbolic act of reconciliation. And the truth: We are all bandits. We've stolen California from the Mexicans. And they stole it from the Spaniards. And they stole it from the Indians. We can deal with the guilt history places on us only when we free ourselves from the ghosts.

As he speaks, I am struck by how thoroughly a Californian this man is. Alberto Huerta grew up in Fairfield. He recalls a small agricultural town of the 1940s. He recalls a "Mediterranean world," a California attentive to seasons and to weather. "It is a cliché in the East to say that there are no seasons in California. They mean flowers and snow. But Californians are conscious of seasons through crops. We tell time by the vegetables and fruits in the supermarket. Asparagus means spring; apricots and peaches are summer; grapes in the fall."

Fairfield was a Catholic town; people were Portuguese or Mexican, Italian or Basque. "Travis Air Force Base was new then. Travis brought new people into our world; we regarded them with respect, but with suspicion."

California was changing in those postwar years. "But I still think of myself now as a *californio*," Huerta says, using the old Spanish word. He is, he insists, from *here*.

"Someday I want people to read my work and say not that I was Mexican or American but that I lived in the shadow of the missions."

Here? In the Balboa Cafe? *In the shadow of the missions?* That phrase preoccupies him. His enthusiasm for California is based on his sense of its difference. Hispanic culture took root here. "People came west in later generations, and even when the old culture was in ruins—the missions in ruins—they recognized the Mediterranean." Memory survived to instruct the newcomer. "Easterners who have grown up in a Puritan culture joke about 'laid-back' California. They do not understand. California is Latin—there is a different sense of leisure here and a freedom from busy-ness."

Father Huerta believes in the power of memory. Californians are linked by memory—mainly unconscious—to a founding Hispanic culture. In homage to that memory, Huerta writes scholarly articles in Spanish and sends them off to Madrid to be published. It is not that he repudiates Anglo-California; it is rather this matter of shadows.

■ ■ ■

Father Huerta is driving. We have just passed Stonestown, a section of San Francisco I don't know very well. We are going to meet a man named Sig Christopherson, "the Mexican Sigui." Surely an ironic sobriquet? Huerta says not.

The front door is wide open. We ring the bell. Sig Christopherson is a big man in his sixties. He welcomes me with a slap on the shoulder, more of a Westerner than one is accustomed to meeting in San Francisco. On the front-room walls are photographs of children or grandchildren; black sombreros with white tracery; posters announcing the appearance of some Mexican singer in a Valley town. The dining-room table is stacked with Mexican cowboy records and with books on the Old West; on another table I notice the handle of a knife, a rusty gun, some bullets. Sig Christopherson is in the construction business; he also sells real estate.

Christopherson was born a world away, in Manitoba, a tiny community of Icelandic immigrants ("Maybe that's why I know something about being a minority"). He came to California as a young man, loved the land, raised horses, got to know Mexicans in Valley towns. He stayed, became a Californian—easy enough to do—but Christopherson was never a gringo, never a stranger.

Father Huerta explains that Christopherson has lobbied the state legislature to include the Arroyo Cantua in a land purchase it is considering in Fresno County under Senate Bill 1264. The state wants to use the land for recreational vehicles. Sig Christopherson wants the Arroyo Cantua fenced off, the buildings on the site preserved in honor of the men who were killed there over a century ago. The Arroyo Cantua was the site of a shoot-out (more likely an ambush) involving state rangers and a Mexican band of horse robbers in 1853. At least four Mexicans were killed, and one of the corpses—taken for Joaquín Murrieta—was beheaded.

Christopherson is well known to Sacramento legislators. For years he has worked to exonerate the name of Joaquín Murrieta. ("The man was never tried.") Christopherson has lobbied to remove Historical Marker 344, which identifies the Arroyo Cantua as the site of the death of "the notorious bandit, Joaquín Murrieta." On May 2, 1983, an earthquake hit the nearby town of Coalinga. The quake's epicenter was directly beneath state marker 344 (God's bull's-eye?). "The state had to come and cart the rubble away," Sigui chuckles with satisfaction.

The Mexican Sigui has become a kind of priest of the Mexican side, the occult side, of the Murrieta myth. Throughout the Central Valley, people have seen Joaquín ride at night. A blue horseman, they say. Or a green horseman kicking up dust storms on windless nights. Accidents on Pacheco Pass—cars swerving to avoid hitting men on horseback suddenly projected by headlamps onto the fog. Christopherson remembers a summer night in the 1970s, in Eagle Field, when he and some Mexican friends were sitting outside after a bar had closed. Around four in the morning, they heard the music of Mexican guitars from inside the locked cantina.

They could see candles flickering behind the curtained windows.

This is the part of the Murrieta myth that drives historians crazy. But it is an essential part. Legends intrigue or they die.

Legend has it that most of the rangers in Captain Love's posse met bad ends. Love ("the Black Knight of Zayante") died in a shoot-out with his wife's lover. The ranger named Bill Byrnes, who cut off the hand of Three-Fingered Jack and chopped off the head of the man taken to be Joaquín, ended up in the insane asylum in Stockton—a cowboy Macbeth.

The hand in the jar. The head. Here is the strangest part of the story. Within hours of their return, the state rangers exchanged their bloody relics for reward money. Newspaper reporters of the time were skeptical about the authenticity of the dreadful pickles. Who could be sure this was Murrieta's head?

In Frank Latta's history, the captured head is proposed to be that of an Indian named Chappo who rode with Murrieta's band and tended the horses. Murrieta, according to Latta, was elsewhere on that July morning in 1853, but died shortly after of gunshot wounds. Latta believes Joaquín lies buried somewhere in Niles Canyon.

For the next few years, the head from the Arroyo Cantua toured California and was displayed in mining-camp saloons for a dollar. The head, or another head, found its way to Dr. Jordan's Pacific Museum of Anatomy and Science on Market Street in San Francisco, where it remained alongside kangaroos in canisters and Egyptian mummies and the "amazing cyclops child." One April morning in 1906, the lid of the jar began to rattle; the head revolved in its brine. The jar with the head and all the other jars moved on their shelves, then crashed to the ground. It was the Great San Francisco Earthquake. A hideous stew bubbled on the floor for several days as the city burned. Dr. Jordan's Museum did not burn down, but it never reopened. A janitor mopped up the gore and it all got thrown away or was buried somewhere. So they say.

In April, 1980, Sig Christopherson arranged for a Catholic priest, Father Joseph McAllister, to go to 1051 Market Street, the site of the museum. They got keys from the owner of the property and went down to the cellar, where the priest blessed the soil. Up to that time, Christopherson says, there had been a succession of fires in the building. For a time, too, the building was boarded up and someone had spray-painted the words LE-GIONNAIRE'S DISEASE on the plywood covering the door. "That's the disease connected with the curse of King Tut's tomb," Sigui explains.

Every year now, the Mexican Sigui leads a "pilgrimage" to what he calls the "Divine Monument of the Arroyo Cantua." The procession, mostly of Mexican families, gathers outside Our Lady of Guadalupe Church in Three Rocks, California, on the last Sunday of July. The event is covered by Spanish-language radio stations. A priest recites some prayers. There are horse tricks and music; kids wear themselves out. A Fresno Coors distributor sends out a truckload of free beer.

■ ■ ■

The red light of my answering machine is blinking again. It is Father Huerta again. *"Thees—ees—the-head-of-Hwa-keen-Moo-rree-et-tah."*

Then in his real voice: He has found the head. It is in Santa Rosa. It belongs to a man named Walter Johnson, an ornamental-rock salesman who paid twenty-five hundred dollars for it several years ago. Johnson ran a kind of Old West museum for a time.

Enough already! I don't want anything more to do with this stuff. I erase the tape and turn on Johnny Carson's monologue. But in the morning I phone Father Huerta.

A few days later, he drives up in his oversize Jesuit Chevy.

145

He is in a playful mood, but he is wearing his black suit and clerical collar. He has telephoned ahead. One of the Johnson boys will be home. He hums the four notes of the *Dragnet* theme as we buckle up.

Santa Rosa is an hour away. We pass the time—miles of "great-deal condominiums" and "deluxe" office buildings and tile-roofed shopping centers—talking about anything but Joaquín Murrieta's head.

We reach the turnoff. I have an address in my hand. We drive slowly and we find the place only after first passing it. (The address of the building on the left is too high; the place on the right is too low.) We come back—there is no number.

There is a road. We drive toward a small brown house surrounded by boulders. A pickup truck is parked at the side. When Father Huerta stops the car, there is only the sound of the engine ticking cool.

"After you, señor." (Boris Karloff.) But when I look, Huerta is not smiling.

We get out. We walk toward the house. There are children's toys in the path. I think to myself of the climactic scene in *Lord of the Flies*. Stop it, I tell myself. But when I look over to Father Huerta, he seems dressed now for some sort of exorcism.

I knock. I knock again.

No answer.

Father Huerta calls out: "Hello?"

We hear some footsteps within. The door opens.

Dogs. Four or five of them in a Cerberus-knot are sniffing at us. They don't make a sound. Behind the dogs is a man. Yes, he knows who we are. His name is Bill Johnson—the son. He wears jeans and a T-shirt. He is good-looking, unshaven; a kind face. His eyes are red. (Has he been sleeping? It is just after one.)

The Head of Joaquín Murrieta

No sooner are we in the front room than my eye finds the jar with the head, on top of a safe in the corner. Disappointing, at first, like the *Mona Lisa*. Bill Johnson goes and picks it up and brings it over to the Formica table in the center of the room.

I look away. The room is a mess. There are artifacts, some Indian things from Johnson's Old West Museum. To the right is a doorway leading back, probably to the kitchen. A dark stairway. Everywhere there are flies circling. And sniffer-dogs at my legs. To move at all is to wade through dog.

Bill Johnson explains that he lives here with a brother. His parents have moved away. Perhaps this is only the mess two brothers make? But I am convinced the head has brought the disorder. Everything seems to be in the wrong place. A bowl of dog food is on the table. There are pillows on the floor.

Bill Johnson stands aside, the docent, watching Father Huerta watching me. Johnson says the house is no longer a museum, but there are still people who have heard about the head and come by for a look. Father Huerta notices a crack on the upper lip. "Oh yeah," Johnson says. "In the old days, they used to put a kind of mortician's clay on the body to preserve it."

Huerta had already warned me that some people think this head is a fake—not human. But if this is a joke on the memory of a dead man, the dead man seems still to be plotting revenge. The dark hair floats like sea grass.

The eyes are open.

"We've had an undertaker look at the head," Bill Johnson replies, as if the dogs had relayed a skeptical scent. "He said you can tell from the eyes that the guy had a violent death."

Father Huerta is circling the jar; he pulls out a camera and begins to take pictures.

A family lived in this room. People ate here, laughed, presumably. The Johnsons have a daughter, I learn, who brings her children to the house. "Did it ever bother you to have this head around?" I ask.

"Naw," he says. "I've seen it all my life. It's kind of like a piece of furniture—an antique."

So there really was such a place as the Wild West. There was a time in California when something sprang loose in the soul. And here in this two-bit museum in Santa Rosa that time is memorialized.

"My father has some Indian skulls upstairs, if you want to take a look," Bill Johnson says.

Father Huerta looks pale, his voice a murmur. "If you—if your father is ever interested in giving up this head," he says, "I will be glad to take it and see it gets buried."

Johnson says nothing. He stares. We thank him. He nods. We shake hands. When we are outside, a white van passes on the road and a pale face sticks out, passenger side, to yell something, laughing. (What?)

"Did you notice?" Father Huerta asks as we drive onto the freeway. "The head is expanding. I think it's going to explode."

I imagine the explosion of the hideous piñata rocking the mission church at Santa Clara. The governor. "Dies Irae." Joan Baez. Sombreros in the air.

We are driving now past Novato, approaching San Rafael. I can tell from the traffic that it's getting late. Neither of us wants the lunch we had planned for the way back. Marin County housewives, zombielike at the wheels of their BMWs, surround us, an honor guard back to the land of the living.

Just before we get to the Golden Gate Bridge, Father Huerta interrupts our silence. "Somebody should bury that thing."

CHAPTER SEVEN

Sand

The prize for selling 146 subscriptions to the *Catholic Herald* was a red bicycle and a trip to Disneyland.

I wasn't all that thrilled about Disneyland. Yet I remember walking back from the six o'clock mass with my father that morning; the summer morning's silence; the sense of moment. I had never been more than a hundred miles from Sacramento; I had never stayed in a motel.

I rode shotgun alongside Mr. Kelley, the *Herald*'s circulation manager. The second-place winner from Holy Spirit (one hundred subscriptions) sat in the back seat.

All the way down Highway 99, past the truck stops, the Dairy Queens, the Giant Oranges, past Modesto and Fresno and the turnoffs to hundreds of country roads, in between the yes-pleases and no-thank-yous, we listened to "Monitor"—the weekend service of NBC Radio. Each hour passed with the announcer's intoning from Rockefeller Center: "This is 'Monitor,' going places, doing things."

There had been a typhoon in Asia. Each time the static receded, more green bodies had washed up among the baseball scores. I stared out the car window, dreaming of Rockefeller Center.

Great cities were tall cities. New York promised most glamour for being the tallest, the coolest, the farthest from these even rows of green; this hot, flat Valley floor.

In the late 1950s, it was still possible to imagine Times Square outside the studio—rain-slickened Broadway awash with neon— and the taxicab that brought Miss Arlene Francis to the theater.

Billy Reckers sent me a postcard from L.A. once—white, horizontal, vast—a vast Sacramento. The house where Gracie Allen lived on TV looked like the houses on 45th Street. The streets on *Dragnet* looked like the streets downtown.

But on two festival days, Los Angeles seemed more glamorous than anywhere else in the world.

New Year's Day was blind and cold in Sacramento. We had the tule fog. We chastened our rooms and our memories, replaced the Christmas ornaments in their cardboard boxes, labeled the boxes, packed them away. On our black-and-white television screen, it was always bright for the Rose Parade from sunny Pasadena, the sunlight dancing on chrome, sunlight flashing from the rhinestones of the Rose Queen and her court.

On the night of the Academy Awards, movie stars pretended real lives, getting out of limousines, walking the gauntlet of flash bulbs. Cleopatra, Tarzan, Mrs. Miniver were all neighbors, all lived in ranch-style houses in L.A.

Mr. Kelley got us to Los Angeles by six o'clock, as he had promised. (We'll stop for dinner, stay overnight in a motel in Hollywood; then drive to Disneyland in the morning.)

Was this it? Even Sacramento had its ceremonial entrance, over the Tower Bridge. After the long, straight line of Highway 99 and the drama of the Tehachapi Mountains—ten hours—we had undergone no change. We drove along Sepulveda Boulevard, looking for a place to eat.

We parked under the aerodynamic roof of a restaurant that looked like a butterfly. I ordered "chicken in the basket."

We found a motel near the famous Hollywood Bowl. We got one room with twin beds. Mr. Kelley took one of the beds. I shared mine with the runner-up from Holy Spirit. We watched *Lawrence Welk*, because Mr. Kelley's uncle was famous. Mr. Kelley's uncle played the champagne organ. Mr. Kelley wandered around the room in his boxer shorts, scratching. I studied the hair on Mr. Kelley's back as he talked to his wife on the telephone.

A few years later, Johnny Carson moved *The Tonight Show* from New York to Los Angeles. Carson told jokes that began with freeways as the metaphor for American innocence, for minding one's own business, for being abroad in the great world ("I was driving along the Ventura Freeway the other day . . .").

By that time, Los Angeles had become the capital of America. By that time, most of America looked like L.A.

■   ■   ■

I moved to Los Angeles when I was twenty-eight. The part of the city I knew was the west side, the famous side, from West Hollywood to Santa Monica, north along the coast to Malibu and south to the Palisades. The west side did not define Los Angeles any more than Pasadena did. Pasadena was also Los Angeles and Burbank was also Los Angeles and Torrance and Watts, Glendale, Tarzana, Boyle Heights.

Los Angeles had not yet undergone its metamorphosis—not yet the Pacific Rim capital, crowded with immigrants, choking on tragedy. Los Angeles was a Protestant dream of a city, a low city: separate houses, separate lawns, separate cars. Los Angeles was famous among American cities for being the creation of native-born Americans—"internal immigrants" from Iowa or from Brooklyn. Its tone was comic. Its scale was childish—giant donuts and eight-lane freeways. Los Angeles was not the creation of foreign parents escaping tragedy; Los Angeles was the creation of American children.

People I knew on the west side rarely went to the Mexican side. People in the San Fernando Valley expressed fatuous pride at not having been downtown for years. Orange County was the region's largest attempt to secede from itself. But Los Angeles named everything and everyone, claimed every horizon. The city without a center was everywhere the city. L.A. bestowed metropolitan stature on the suburban.

America made fun of L.A.

Europeans admired, especially Brits admired Los Angeles.

In London, I met a specimen of one of England's most congealed bloods who was disappointed to learn that I was from San Francisco, oh dear—he much preferred *Los Annjilleeze*.

In 1971, Reynor Banham, a British architectural critic, published his pop celebration of the city, *Los Angeles: The Architecture of Four Ecologies*. Banham wrote disparagingly of the California alternative—San Francisco—with its "prefabricated Yankee houses and prefabricated New England or European attitudes."

Then David Hockney arrived in L.A. from coal-blackened northern England; dyed his hair, changed into shorts; eased into a primary palette. Hockney sold his canvas to the world: suburban tract villas, blond statue boys, an Aqua Velva Mediterranean.

Europe sought freedom from centuries. Europe craved vulgarity. Europe found innocence.

For all its innocence, L.A. was flattered by Europe's attentions in those years. It was the stuff of sonnets—old men taking young men to the opera at the Dorothy Chandler Pavilion. In a way, Europe was turning a trick on L.A., teaching the capital of childish narcissism the confidence of outward regard. L.A. soon came to believe that it was indeed an important city, a world city. "London, Paris, Beverly Hills," read the perfume bottles. British actors and German divas were flown into town like so many truffles. In return, Los Angeles opened the last great European museum in the world, an authentic Greek temple at the edge of the sea.

I imagined I knew some secret about Los Angeles that other people did not know. The architect who Bauhaused his bungalow was living in a house identical to the house I had grown up in. The Sacramento boy still refused to believe that a horizontal city could be a great city. But there were times when Los Angeles amused me for taking all I dismissed as Sacramento and selling it to the world as glamour. What a joke!

I now realize that Los Angeles was doing the same with me. I was a Mexican from the Central Valley—even then L.A. was the second-largest Mexican city in the world—a Mexican kid from the Central Valley with a big nose and glasses. I had spent my life indoors, reading about London.

But in L.A. I passed for a glamour-boy.

"Because you can talk," one angel explained. "All they want is to be amused."

I had always been intellectually arrogant. In L.A., I yearned to become glamorous enough to be humble, in the manner of the angels.

There was nothing reticent about L.A. Glamour was instant. The city took its generosity from the movies. You're beautiful if L.A. says you're beautiful, goddammit.

It was the sons of Jewish immigrants, the haberdasher's son and the tobacconist's son, who established the epic scale of the movies. Movies taught one big lesson: individual lives have scope and grandeur.

Of course L.A. is shallow. Lips that are ten feet long and faces that are forty feet high! But such faces magnify our lives, reassure us that single lives matter. The attention L.A. lavishes on a single face is as generous a metaphor as I can find for the love of God.

My favorite time in the city was twilight, when theater lights dim, when the curtain opens. Then the basin of L.A. released its cocktail scent, lacrimatory, grenadine, rose. I flew through the brimstone canyons in a borrowed convertible, heedless, drum-driven.

To my first L.A. party. Some gallery opening on Melrose. A Scandinavian diplomat stands all alone with a drink melting in his hand. The gallery is too crowded, too noisy. I have to shout my name in the diplomat's ear. A golden ear, like a scroll.

Who was that? the Scandinavian diplomat later asked the gallery owner, who still later told me this story.

"You mean the professional tennis player?" The owner shrugged, confusing me with one of the Bombay brothers then on the international circuit.

(My first role.)

I became a writer in L.A. I jogged, I house-sat, I watched dragonflies patrol swimming pools. I turned the pages of fashion magazines.

I went apartment-hunting in Santa Monica. The real-estate agent drove me in her borrowed convertible to an apartment not far from the beach. The carpet was rust-colored shag. An aluminum sliding glass door led to a redwood deck overlooking the garage. Dark-green plants were suspended in papooses of hemp. The previous tenant had left the kitchen cupboard filled with neatened piles of *Playboy*.

"It only needs . . . ?" the real-estate agent prompted.

There is a picture of me, taken one afternoon at the UCLA track field. I am stretching, standing on one leg like a tropical bird. The spread, when it was published, was titled BOYS OF SUMMER. I was far from being a boy that day, far from the gravity of the twelve-year-old who won Disneyland. And the day was far from a summer's day. It was December 31.

The most depressing time in L.A. is the moment when the screen dies, the theater lights come up. I came out of the theater on Wilshire, my eyes unaccustomed to the light.

Within a month, I am shivering in a thin sports jacket on a pedestrian island in the middle of Market Street in San Francisco. My pants legs are blowing in the wind. Shadows are stumbling around me in the dark, burping into aluminum cans or raging with sacrilege.

I am carrying a suitcase. If the trolley ever comes, I face several months in the basement apartment of my parents' home, completing a book.

The angelic friends told me I was making a mistake.

I told them I could not find a bright enough apartment in L.A. for the price I was willing to pay.

The truth was, I had doubted. The truth was, I didn't have even enough childish imagination to Bauhaus a Santa Monica apartment.

My last L.A. party: a party in Westwood, where I met the idol of my reading life, an extraordinary critic, a superstar among critics, a word-Adonis. Over there, on the sofa by the lamp, someone whispered. What, but here was a little gray man. He crossed his legs like a woman; his trousers were too high; his socks were too low. I noticed the pale hairless shin as he dandled his foot to and fro.

A writer should be at least as glamorous as his calling. What good are all the gauds and greensleeves of Renaissance poetry, what good are all the leggings and ribbons, the codpieces, quivers, circlets of hair, if they make the banquet of a dry little man?

I will stay in Los Angeles forever.

But what good are leggings and ribbons and weight-lifting salons if your soul is the bathroom mirror?

I've got to get out of this town.

For a time in San Francisco, I continued to wear my shirts unbuttoned far down—Aren't you cold? people asked. I astonished a luncheon companion by dipping my fingers into her San Pellegrino water to anoint my hair. But then I left off. I was starting to go bald anyway.

■ ■ ■

Entering the city that day, when I was twenty-eight, I drove down Highway One. If there is a best way to enter Los Angeles, it is this way—from the north and along the Pacific Coast Highway. I drove past Pepperdine, past Malibu, past the gas stations and public beaches. A Saturday afternoon in summer, the great city at play, and the only premonition of tragedy a dab of sun block.

I turned left at Wilshire, passed the statue of Santa Monica pining for her son's conversion.

A few weeks before, I had left graduate school, a sad case in my cotton washpants, my short-sleeved white shirt, my head a well of poetry, a staircase of poetry, and the aforementioned glasses. I was spending the weekend with a college friend, now a professor at UCLA.

I found myself in Beverly Hills. Most of the streets were empty of pedestrians. I got out for a walk.

I paused at the window of a store on Camden. I went inside. No one paid much attention to me. I browsed and I watched. I had never seen people so formally dressed for the sun.

A man behind the counter asked if I wanted anything to drink. I recognized him. A bit actor on television. I . . . cast down my eyes, I asked him about an orange shirt, raising the shirt from the counter with one finger.

"Are you really interested . . . ? All those pins . . ."

I told him I was serious.

And so he unbuttoned the shirt and I put it on.

A second clerk came over and draped a sweater over my shoulders. The two men studied the effect as if I weren't there.

Toooo blue.

The bit actor crossed to a mannequin.

"Don't say no till you've tried it on."

He held the coat with its lining outward to receive my arms. I glanced down at the lapels. Gaudy, black-and-white checks. I didn't dare.

Then I looked into the mirror.

Another man came from behind the counter and placed a straw hat on my head.

"There."

At that moment, the door opened and Cesar Romero walked into the mirror.

"Great-looking coat," he said, tapping my shoulder lightly as he passed.

CHAPTER EIGHT

Asians

For the child of immigrant parents the knowledge comes like a slap: America exists.

America exists everywhere in the city—on billboards; frankly in the smell of burgers and French fries. America exists in the slouch of the crowd, the pacing of traffic lights, the assertions of neon, the cry of freedom overriding the nineteenth-century melodic line.

Grasp the implications of American democracy in a handshake or in a stranger's Jeffersonian "hi." America is irresistible. Nothing to do with choosing.

Our parents came to America for the choices America offers. What the child of immigrant parents knows is that here is inevitability.

A Chinese boy says his high-school teacher is always after him to stand up, speak up, look up. Yeah, but then his father puts him down at home: "Since when have you started looking your father in the eye?"

I'd like you to meet Jimmy Lamm. Mr. Lamm was an architect

in Saigon. Now he is a cabbie in San Francisco. Stalled in traffic in San Francisco, Jimmy tells me about the refugee camp in Guam where, for nearly two years, he and his family were quartered before their flight to America. A teenager surfs by on a skateboard, his hair cresting in purple spikes like an iron crown, his freedom as apparent, as deplorable, as Huck Finn's.

Damn kid. Honk. Honk.

The damn kid howls with pleasure. Flips us the bird.

Do you worry that your children will end up with purple hair?

Silence.

Then Jimmy says his children have too much respect for the struggle he and his wife endured. His children would never betray him so.

On the floor of Jimmy Lamm's apartment, next to the television, is a bowl of fruit and a burning wand of joss.

He means: his children would never *choose* to betray him.

Immigrant parents re-create a homeland in the parlor, tacking up postcards or calendars of some impossible blue—lake or sea or sky.

The child of immigrant parents is supposed to perch on a hyphen, taking only the dose of America he needs to advance in America.

At the family picnic, the child wanders away from the spiced food and faceless stories to watch some boys playing baseball in the distance.

■ ■ ■

My Mexican father still regards America with skepticism from the high window of his morning paper. "Too much freedom," he says. Though he has spent most of his life in this country, my father yet doubts such a place as the United States of America exists. He cannot discern boundaries. How else to describe a country?

159

My father admires a flower bed on a busy pedestrian street in Zurich—he holds up the *National Geographic* to show me. "You couldn't have that in America," my father says.

When I was twelve years old, my father said he wished his children had Chinese friends—so polite, so serious are Chinese children in my father's estimation. The Spanish word he used was *formal*.

I didn't have any Chinese friends. My father did. Seventh and J Street was my father's Orient. My father made false teeth for several Chinese dentists downtown. When a Chinese family tried to move in a few blocks away from our house, I heard a friend's father boast that the neighbors had banded together to "keep out the Japs."

Many years pass.

In college, I was reading *The Merchant of Venice*—Shylock urging his daughter to avoid the temptation of the frivolous Christians on the lido. Come away from the window, Shylock commands. I heard my father's voice:

> *Hear you me, Jessica.*
> *Lock up my doors, and when you hear the drum*
> *And the vile squealing of the wry-necked fife,*
> *Clamber not you up to the casements then,*
> *Nor thrust your head into the public street*
> *To gaze on Christian fools with varnished faces,*
> *But stop my house's ears, I mean my casements.*
> *Let not the sound of shallow foppery enter*
> *My sober house.*

■ ■ ■

I interview the mother on Evergreen Street for the *Los Angeles Times*. The mother says they came from Mexico ten years ago, and—look—already they have this nice house. Each year the kitchen takes on a new appliance.

Outside the door is Los Angeles; in the distance, the perpetual orbit of traffic. Here old women walk slowly under paper parasols, past the Vietnam vet who pushes his tinkling ice-cream cart past little green lawns, little green lawns, little green lawns. (Here teenagers have black scorpions tattooed into their biceps.)

Children here are fed and grow tall. They love Christmas. They laugh at cartoons. They go off to school with children from Vietnam, from Burbank, from Hong Kong. They get into fights. They come home and they say dirty words. Aw, Ma, they say. Gimme a break, they say.

The mother says she does not want American children. It is the thing about Los Angeles she fears, the season of adolescence, of Huck Finn and Daisy Miller.

Foolish mother. She should have thought of that before she came. She will live to see that America takes its meaning from adolescence. She will have American children.

■ ■ ■

The best metaphor of America remains the dreadful metaphor—the Melting Pot. Fall into the Melting Pot, ease into the Melting Pot, or jump into the Melting Pot—it makes no difference—you will find yourself a stranger to your parents, a stranger to your own memory of yourself.

A Chinese girl walks to the front of the classroom, unfolds several ruled pages, and begins to read her essay to a trio of judges (I am one of her judges).

The voice of the essay is the voice of an immigrant. Stammer and elision approximate naïveté (the judges squirm in their chairs). The narrator remembers her night-long journey to the United States aboard a Pan Am jet. The moon. Stars. Then a memory within a memory: in the darkened cabin of the plane, sitting next to her sleeping father, the little girl remembers bright China.

Many years pass.

The narrator's voice hardens into an American voice; her diction takes on rock and chrome. There is an ashtray on the table. The narrator is sitting at a sidewalk café in San Francisco. She is sixteen years old. She is with friends. The narrator notices a Chinese girl passing on the sidewalk. The narrator remembers bright China. The passing girl's face turns toward hers. The narrator recognizes herself in the passing girl—herself less assimilated. Their connective glance lasts only seconds. The narrator is embarrassed by her double—she remembers the cabin of the plane, her sleeping father, the moon, stars. The stranger disappears.

End of essay.

The room is silent as the Chinese student raises her eyes from the text.

One judge breaks the silence. Do you think your story is a sad story?

No, she replies. It is a true story.

What is the difference?

(Slowly, then.)

When you hear a sad story you cry, she says. When you hear a true story you cry even more.

■ ■ ■

The U.S. Army took your darling boy, didn't they? With all his allergies and his moles and his favorite flavors. And when they gave him back, the crystals of his eyes had cracked. You weren't sure if this was the right baby. The only other institution as unsentimental and as subversive of American individuality has been the classroom.

Asians

In the nineteenth century, even as the American city was building, Samuel Clemens romanced the nation with a celebration of the wildness of the American river, the eternal rejection of school and shoes. But in the red brick cities, and on streets without trees, the river became an idea, a learned idea, a shared idea, a civilizing idea, taking all to itself. Women, usually women, stood in front of rooms crowded with the children of immigrants, teaching those children a common language. For language is not just another classroom skill, as today's bilingualists would have it. Language is *the* lesson of grammar school. And from the schoolmarm's achievement came the possibility of a shared history and a shared future. To my mind, this achievement of the nineteenth-century classroom was an honorable one, comparable to the opening of the plains, the building of bridges. Grammar-school teachers forged a nation.

A century later, my own teachers encouraged me to read *Huckleberry Finn*. I tried several times. My attempts were frustrated by the dialect voices. (*You don't know about me without you have read* . . .) There was, too, a confidence in Huck I shied away from and didn't like and wouldn't trust. The confidence was America.

Eventually, but this was many years after, I was able to read in Huck's dilemma—how he chafed so in autumn—a version of my own fear of the classroom: Huck as the archetypal bilingual child. And, later still, I discerned in Huck a version of the life of our nation.

This nation was formed from a fear of the crowd. Those early Puritans trusted only the solitary life. Puritans advised fences. Build a fence around all you hold dear and respect other fences. Protestantism taught Americans to believe that America does not exist—not as a culture, not as shared experience, not as a communal reality. Because of Protestantism, the American *ideology*

163

of individualism is always at war with the experience of our lives, our *culture*. As long as we reject the notion of culture, we are able to invent the future.

Lacking any plural sense of ourselves, how shall we describe Americanization, except as loss? The son of Italian immigrant parents is no longer Italian. America is the country where one stops being Italian or Chinese or German.

And yet notice the testimony of thousands of bellhops in thousands of hotel lobbies around the world: Americans exist. There is a recognizable type—the accent, of course; the insecure tip; the ready smile; the impatience; the confidence of an atomic bomb informing every gesture.

When far from home, Americans easily recognize one another in a crowd. It is only when we return home, when we live and work next to one another, that Americans choose to believe anew in the fact of our separateness.

Americans have resorted to the idea of a shared culture only at times of international competition; at times of economic depression; during war; during periods of immigration. Nineteenth-century nativists feared Catholics and Jews would undermine the Protestant idea of America. As the nineteenth-century American city crowded with ragpickers, and crucifix-kissers, and garlic-eaters, yes, and as metaphors of wildness attached to the American city, nativists consoled themselves with a cropped version of America—the small white town, the general store, the Elks Hall, the Congregational church.

To this day, political journalists repair to the "heartland" to test the rhetoric of Washington or New York against true America.

But it was the antisociability of American Protestantism which paradoxically allowed for an immigrant nation. Lacking a communal sense, how could Americans resist the coming of strangers?

America became a multiracial, multireligious society precisely because a small band of Puritans did not want the world.

The American city became the fame of America worldwide.

In time, the American city became the boast of America. In time, Americans would admit their country's meaning resided in the city. America represented freedom—the freedom to leave Europe behind, the freedom to re-create one's life, the freedom to re-create the world. In time, Americans came to recognize themselves in the immigrant—suitcase in hand, foreign-speaking, bewildered by the city. The figure of the immigrant became, like the American cowboy, a figure of loneliness, and we trusted that figure as descriptive of Protestant American experience. We are a nation of immigrants, we were able to say.

Now "Hispanics and Asians" have replaced "Catholics and Jews" in the imaginations of nativists. The nativist fear is that non-European immigrants will undo the European idea of America (forgetting that America was formed against the idea of Europe).

We are a nation of immigrants—most of us say it easily now. And we are working on a new cliché to accommodate new immigrants: the best thing about immigrants, the best that they bring to America, we say, is their "diversity." We mean they are not us—the Protestant creed.

■   ■   ■

In the late nineteenth century, when much of San Francisco was sand dunes, city fathers thought to plant a large park running out to the edge of the sea. Prescient city fathers. San Francisco would become crowded. Someday there would be the need for a park at the edge of the sea.

Having reached the end of the continent, Americans contemplated finitude. The Pacific Coast was ominous to the California imagination. The Pacific Coast was an Asian horizon. The end of us was the beginning of them. Old duffers warned, "Someday there will be sampans in the harbor."

With one breath people today speak of Hispanics and Asians —the new Americans. Between the two, Asians are the more admired—the model minority—more protestant than Protestants; so hardworking, self-driven; so bright. But the Asian remains more unsettling to American complacence, because the Asian is culturally more foreign.

Hispanics may be reluctant or pushy or light or dark, but Hispanics are recognizably European. They speak a European tongue. They worship or reject a European God. The shape of the meat they eat is identifiable. But the Asian?

Asians rounded the world for me. I was a Mexican teenager in America who had become an Irish Catholic. When I was growing up in the 1960s, I heard Americans describing their nation as simply bipartate: black and white. When black and white America argued, I felt I was overhearing some family quarrel that didn't include me. Korean and Chinese and Japanese faces in Sacramento rescued me from the simplicities of black and white America.

I was in high school when my uncle from India died, my Uncle Raj, the dentist. After Raj died, we went to a succession of Chinese dentists, the first Asian names I connected with recognizable faces; the first Asian hands.

In the 1960s, whole blocks of downtown Sacramento were to be demolished for a redevelopment. The *Sacramento Bee* reported several Chinese businessmen had declared their intention to build a ten-story office building downtown with a pagoda roof. About that same time, there was another article in the *Bee*. Mexican entrepreneurs would turn Sixth and K into a Mexican block with cobblestones, restaurants, colonial façades. My father was skeptical concerning the Mexican enterprise. "Guess which one will never get built?" my father intoned from the lamplight, snapping the spine of his newspaper.

Dr. Chiang, one of our family dentists, had gone to the University of the Pacific. He encouraged the same school for me. Our entire conversational motif, repeated at every visit, was college—his path and my plans.

Then there was Dr. Wang.

Not Dr. Wang! My sister refused. Dr. Wang didn't bother with Novocaine. Dr. Wang's office was a dark and shabby place.

My father said we owed it to Dr. Wang to be his patients. Dr. Wang referred business to my father.

Dr. Wang joked about my long nose. "Just like your father." And again: "Just like your father," as he pulled my nose up to open my mouth. Then China entered my mouth in a blast of garlic, a whorl of pain.

The Chinese businessmen built a ten-story office building downtown with a pagoda roof. Just as my father predicted they would.

■　■　■

Americans must resist the coming of fall, the starched shirt, the inimical expectation of the schoolmarm, because Americans want to remain individual. The classroom will teach us a language in common. The classroom will teach a history that implicates us with others. The classroom will tell us that we belong to a culture.

American educators, insofar as they are Americans, share with their students a certain ambivalence, even a resistance, to the public lessons of school. Witness the influence of progressivism on American education, a pedagogy that describes the primary purpose of education as fostering independence of thought, creativity, originality—notions that separate one student from another.

The hardest lesson for me, as for Huck Finn, as for the Chinese kid in the fifth paragraph of this chapter, was the lesson of public identity. What I needed from the classroom was a public life. The earliest necessity for any student is not individuality but something closer to the reverse. With Huck, I needed to learn the names of British kings and dissident Protestants, because they were the beginning of us. I read the writings of eighteenth-century white men who powdered their wigs and kept slaves, because these were the men who shaped the country that shaped my life.

Today Huck Finn would emerge as the simple winner in the contest of public education. Today Huck's schoolmarm would be cried down by her students as a tyrannical supremacist.

American educators have lost the confidence of their public institution. The failure represents, in part, an advance for America: the advance of the postwar black civil-rights movement. As America became racially integrated, Americans were less inclined to claim a common identity. It was easier to speak of an American "we" when everyone in the classroom was the same color. And then, as America became integrated, the black civil-rights movement encouraged a romantic secession from the idea of America—Americans competed with one another to claim victimization for themselves, some fence for themselves as minorities.

A second factor undermining the classroom's traditional function has been the large, non-European immigration of the last two decades. It was one thing to imagine a common culture when most immigrants came from Europe. A grammar-school teacher in California may now have students from fifty-four language groups in her class, as does one grammar-school teacher I know. How shall she teach such an assembly anything singular?

Or the college professor who lectures on Shakespeare. Most of his students are Asian. He was grading papers on *The Merchant of Venice* last term when he suddenly realized most of his Asian students had no idea what it meant that Shylock was a Jew.

Teachers and educational bureaucrats bleat in chorus: we are a nation of immigrants. The best that immigrants bring to America is diversity. American education should respect diversity, celebrate diversity. Thus the dilemma of our national diversity becomes (with a little choke on logic) the solution to itself. But diversity is a liquid noun. Diversity admits everything, stands for nothing.

There are influential educators today, and I have met them, who believe the purpose of American education is to instill in children a pride in their ancestral pasts. Such a curtailing of education seems to me condescending; seems to me the worst sort of missionary spirit. Did anyone attempt to protect the white middle-class student of yore from the ironies of history? Thomas Jefferson—that great democrat—was also a slaveowner. Need we protect black students from complexity? Thomas Jefferson, that slaveowner, was also a democrat. American history has become a pageant of exemplary slaves and black educators. Gay studies, women's studies, ethnic studies—the new curriculum ensures that education will be flattering. But I submit that America is not a tale for sentimentalists.

If I am a newcomer to your country, why teach me about my ancestors? I need to know about seventeenth-century Puritans in order to make sense of the rebellion I notice everywhere in the American city. Teach me about mad British kings so I will understand the American penchant for iconoclasm. Then teach me about cowboys and Indians; I should know that tragedies created the country that will create me.

Once you toss out Benjamin Franklin and Andrew Jackson,

you toss out Navajos. You toss out immigrant women who worked the sweatshops of the Lower East Side. Once you toss out Thomas Jefferson, you toss out black history.

A high-school principal tells me there are few black students in his school, but—oh my!—in the last decade his school has changed its color, changed its accent; changed memory. Instead of Black History Week, his school now observes "Newcomers' Week." But does not everyone in America have a stake in black history? To be an American is to belong to black history.

To argue for a common culture is not to propose an exclusionary culture or a static culture. The classroom is always adding to the common text, because America is a dynamic society. Susan B. Anthony, Martin Luther King, Jr., are inducted into the textbook much as they are canonized by the U.S. Postal Service, not as figures of diversity, but as persons who implicate our entire society.

Sherlock Holmes?

I know a lot of teachers. Yet another teacher faces an eighth-grade class of Filipino immigrants. Boy-oh-boy, she would sure like to watch me try to teach her eighth-grade Filipino students to read Conan Doyle.

For example, she says: Meerschaum—a kind of pipe. Well, a pipe—you know, you smoke? Pen knife. Bell pull. Harley Street. Hobnail boots. Dressing gown. Fez. Cockney. Turkish delight. Pall Mall. Wales . . . Well, they know what whales are, she says mordantly. It's too hard. It's too hard for Conan Doyle, that's for damn sure.

But for Shakespeare?

A high-school counselor tells me her school will soon be without a football team. Too few whites and blacks are enrolled; Hispanic and Asian kids would rather play soccer. As I listen to her, a thought occurs to me: she hates football. She looks for the demise of football. Perhaps what she wants most from Hispanic and Asian children is the same reassurance earlier generations of Americans sought from European immigrants, the reassurance—the hope— that an immigrant can undo America, can untie the cultural knot.

Now the American university is dismantling the American canon in my name. In the name of my father, in the name of Chinese grocers and fry cooks and dentists, the American university disregards the Judeo-Christian foundation of the American narrative. The white university never asked my father whether or not his son should read Milton, of course. Hispanics and Asians have become the convenient national excuse for the accomplishment of what America has always wanted done—the severing of memory, the dismantlement of national culture. The end of history.

Americans are lonely now. Hispanics and Asians represent to us the alternatives of communal cultures at a time when Americans are demoralized. Americans are no longer sure that economic invincibility derives from individualism. Look at Japan! Americans learn chopsticks. Americans lustily devour what they say they fear to become. Sushi will make us lean, corporate warriors. Mexican Combination Plate #3, smothered in mestizo gravy, will burn a hole through our hearts.

No belief is more cherished by Americans, no belief is more typical of America, than the belief that one can choose to be free of American culture. One can pick and choose. Learn Spanish. Study Buddhism. . . . My Mexican father was never so American as when he wished his children might cultivate Chinese friends.

■   ■   ■

Many years pass.

Eventually I made my way through *Huckleberry Finn*. I was, by that time, a graduate student of English, able to trail Huck and Jim through thickets of American diction and into a clearing.

171

Sitting in a university library, I saw, once more, the American river.

There is a discernible culture, a river, a thread, connecting Thomas Jefferson to Lucille Ball to Malcolm X to Sitting Bull. The panhandler at one corner is related to the pamphleteer at the next, who is related to the bank executive who is related to the Punk wearing a FUCK U T-shirt. The immigrant child sees this at once. But then he is encouraged to forget the vision.

When I was a boy who spoke Spanish, I saw America whole. I realized that there was a culture here because I lived apart from it. I didn't like America. Then I entered the culture. I entered the culture as you did, by going to school. I became Americanized. I ended up believing in choices as much as any of you do.

What my best teachers realized was their obligation to pass on to their students a culture in which the schoolmarm is portrayed as a minor villain.

■ ■ ■

When I taught Freshman English at Berkeley, I took the "F" bus from San Francisco. This was about the time when American educators were proclaiming Asians to be "whiz kids" and Asian academic triumphs fed the feature pages of American newspapers. There were lots of Asians on the "F" bus.

One day, sitting next to a Chinese student on the bus, I watched him study. The way he worried over the text was troubling to me. He knew something about the hardness of life, the seriousness of youth, that America had never taught me. I turned away; I looked out the bus window; I got off the bus at my usual stop. But consider the two of us on the "F" bus headed for Berkeley: the Chinese student poring over his text against some terrible test. Me sitting next to him, my briefcase full of English novels; lucky me. The Asian and the Hispanic. We represented, so many Americans then imagined, some new force in America, a revolutionary change, an undoing of the European line. But it was not so.

Immigrant parents send their children to school (simply, they think) to acquire the skills to "survive" in America. But the child returns home as America. Foolish immigrant parents.

By eight o'clock that morning—the morning of the bus ride— I stood, as usual, in a classroom in Wheeler Hall, lecturing on tragedy and comedy. Asian kids at the back of the room studied biochemistry, as usual, behind propped-up Shakespeares. I said nothing, made no attempt to recall them. At the end of the hour, I announced to the class that, henceforward, class participation would be a consideration in grading. Asian eyes peered over the blue rims of their Oxford Shakespeares.

Three Asian students came to my office that afternoon. They were polite. They had come to ask about the final exam—what did they need to know?

They took notes. Then one student (I would have said the most Americanized of the three) spoke up: "We think, Mr. Rodriguez, that you are prejudiced against Asian students. Because we do not speak up in class."

I made a face. Nonsense, I blustered. Freshman English is a course concerned with language. Is it so unreasonable that I should expect students to speak up in class? One Asian student is the best student in class . . . and so forth.

I don't remember how our meeting concluded. I recall my deliberation when I gave those three grades. And I think now the students were just. I did have a bias, an inevitable American bias, that favored the talkative student. Like most other American teachers, I equated intelligence with liveliness or defiance.

Another Asian student, a woman, an ethnic Chinese student from Vietnam or Cambodia, ended up with an F in one of my classes. It wasn't that she had no American voice, or even that she didn't know what to make of Thoreau. She had missed too many classes. She didn't even show up for the Final.

On a foggy morning during winter break, this woman came to my office with her father to remonstrate.

I was too embarrassed to look at her. I spoke to her father. She sat by the door.

I explained the five essay assignments. I showed him my grade book, the blank spaces next to her name. The father and I both paused a long time over my evidence. I suggested the university's remedial writing course. . . . *Really, you know, her counselor should never have . . .*

In the middle of my apology, he stood up; he turned and walked to where his daughter sat. I could see only his back as he hovered over her. I heard the slap. He moved away.

And then I saw her. She was not crying. She was looking down at her hands composed neatly on her lap.

Jessica!

CHAPTER NINE

The Latin American Novel

I began to notice storefront churches throughout the Mission District of San Francisco with CRISTO or TEMPLO stenciled in black letters on their marquees. My cousin's wedding was to be held at some such storefront *iglesia*, and the aunts clucked among themselves on the telephone in the evenings: how could she give up the faith of her fathers to become one of those *aleluyas?*

And then I saw Catholic priests in the Central Valley of California distribute signs to their Hispanic parishioners, signs to tape on windows or to tack on doors against the inevitable knock of some evangelical missionary. SOMOS CATOLICOS, the signs read. SOMOS CATOLICOS—a declension of *ser*, to advertise an unchangeable condition, as opposed to *estar*, the changeable. And SOMOS, "we are," because Catholics exist in the plural.

After four Catholic centuries, a new brand of Christianity is catching in the Mission District of San Francisco, in the San Joaquin Valley of California, wherever in the United States there are large populations of Hispanics, and throughout Latin America.

Latin America! The Catholic hemisphere, the last best wine

the Church had counted on to see herself through the twenty-first century—Latin America is turning in its jar to Protestantism. At the beginning of this century, there were fewer than two hundred thousand Protestants in all of Latin America. Today there are more than fifty million Protestants. The rate of conversion leads some demographers to predict Latin America will be Protestant before the end of the next century. Not only Protestant but evangelical.

Evangélico: one who evangelizes; the Christian who preaches the gospel. I use the term loosely to convey a spirit abroad, rather than a church or group of churches. There are evangelical dimensions to all Christian denominations, but those I call evangelical would wish to distinguish themselves from mainline Protestantism, most certainly from Roman Catholicism. Catholics may yet be the most communal of Christians; evangelicals are the most protestant of Protestants.

Evangelicals are fundamentalists. They read scripture literally. Most evangelicals in Latin America are also Pentecostals. Pentecostalism is emotional Christianity, trusting most a condition of enrapturement by the Holy Spirit. Pentecostalism is rife with prophecy, charismata, healings, and the babble of sacred tongues. Evangelical spirituality hinges upon an unmediated experience of Jesus Christ.

Protestantism flourished in Europe in the eighteenth century. Protestantism taught Europe to imagine the self according to a new world of cities. Protestantism taught Europe that the central experience of faith was of the individual standing alone before God.

Protestantism increased fivefold in Latin America in the 1940s. Consider what may be a related statistic concerning Mexico during the 1940s. At the start of the decade, 70 percent of Mexico's population lived in villages of fewer than twenty-five hundred people. Since the 1940s, the population of Mexico has tripled; the countryside has not been able to sustain such life. Seventy percent of the population of Mexico now belongs to the city.

A Mexican priest I know refuses the urgency with which I describe to him the disintegration of Latin American Catholicism. "In Latin America you are Catholic by breathing the air," he says. "The Catholic faith has so permeated the life of the people—the courtroom, the kitchen, the plaza, the architect's eye—it would take centuries for Latin America to sweat all that out."

This is the Catholic way of looking at things. It has been my way. It is as difficult for me to imagine a Protestant Latin America as it is to imagine the Pacific Ocean emptied of salt. Except, of course, that there really was a Protestant Reformation in Europe. The North changed its taste, turned its back on the South—no more golden or blue. Souls changed habit. Statues were broken. Wars were fought and won. And playhouses were locked.

There comes a moment in *Hamlet* that seems to me one of the saddest moments in the world. *Hamlet* stops; Hamlet steps out of his play to address his audience.

Shakespeare no longer believes with Catholic assurance. The traditional faith of the playwright is that we are social creatures; all we need to know about ourselves and about each other we know in communion, in conversation. The play tells all.

When Hamlet leaves the play behind him, *Hamlet* becomes a novel.

■　■　■

"Turn to page 121, line 303: *Let no man in the pride of his horsemanship and his manhood dare to fight alone*. . . . FAHERTY, TAKE OFF THOSE STUPID SUNGLASSES," Brother Michael interjects into the *Iliad*.

Skinny, pale, slouching, Larry Faherty yesterday won the essay contest I had expected, and wanted desperately, to win.

"Faherty, I'll give you three to take them off. ONE . . ."

Our courtship: Larry and I are sitting at the far end of the football field, a blurry distance from the school-yard monitor. Larry uses his milk carton as an ashtray. Larry has been reading a book by James Baldwin about Negroes. Larry Faherty has actually been to New York. Larry Faherty calls Sacramento "Sacramenty." Larry writes poetry, which someday he would like to discuss with me. The farthest I have been is to Mexican border towns to visit relatives. Larry has been to Mexico City to learn Spanish. (The Mexicans spoke to him only in Spanish.) Sometimes Larry makes Mexico sound like a man. We all went down to the whorehouse, he says, flicking an ash. Sometimes he describes Mexico as a woman. Civility is built into the language; a language like lace, he says.

Larry Faherty protests the smallness of our island.

Peter Wagoner, he of the duckling-yellow crew cut and the block sweater, Peter Wagoner warns me in confidence (and for my own good) that Larry Faherty will ruin me . . . "socially." So Larry is jeopardizing my tenuous ties with circles of athletic glamour and social celebrity at school. And my mother worries. My parents are in awe of his parents. Larry's mother is a college professor; his father is high up in the state capitol. My sister Sylvia says yucko—look at his hair—as we watch Larry Faherty sink the kickstand of his bicycle into our front lawn.

Larry Faherty's hair: it is long; it is lacquered with emerald-green Stay-Set. Every four weeks or so, Larry's hair descends over his collar. There is a ritual confrontation in Brother Michael's English class.

"TWO . . ."

Brother Michael is in his twenties, passionate, athletic, sarcastic, the stuff of crushes. Not only does he impart the classics, he plays the lead roles. All the boys think he is their favorite teacher. But he is mine. After school Brother Michael encourages me; he spends time with me; he gets me to write for the school paper. In class I am careful not to act kissy. I am the class wit. Like Falstaff, I take hits and then I hit back. I am as ready to laugh at your humiliation as you are to laugh at mine.

Larry Faherty sits silent. He judges me, I know he does, when I make the class laugh, even at the expense of Brother Michael.

Larry Faherty is the one kid in class I regard as smarter than me. His essays, done the night before, have big words stuck in like cherries. When Larry gets kicked out of class, he is not allowed to come back until he has gone to the barber. Because I am the obedient schoolboy, because I always ask permission, I am fascinated with Larry Faherty's defiance.

"THREE." A rustle of black serge, the little wind of starch and sweat as Brother Michael rushes down my row; a furious slap knocks the sunglasses clattering across the floor.

I, too, laugh when the pneumatic hinge has finally jerked the door shut against Larry. My mother has no reason to fear. I will always be attracted, for the same reason I will never become.

Because I am Catholic.

■ ■ ■

London is a bad place, and there is so little good fellowship, that the next door neighbors don't know one another. Pray give my service to all friends that inquire for me; so I rest
                                        Your loving brother,
                                        Joseph Andrews.

■ ■ ■

The eighteenth-century novel belonged to the city. To London. To Paris. To London. Now Latin America has taken the novel as its genre, and Mexico City, the literary capital of the Latin Americas, is the largest city on earth. A new voice, separated from pastoral memory, finds itself alone, among strangers, with an eccentric story to tell—of misfortune, of blunder and blindest luck. *The reader will scarcely credit how I find myself here.*

An inveterate reader of novels, I have come to the Mission District of San Francisco to witness an evangelical prayer service. I take a folding chair at the back of a high-school gymnasium. My eye that craves narrative—that part of me that seeks to uncover privacy, that part of me that admits afternoon TV talk shows—Protestantism has brought me here.

This is the famous "Junkie Church"—Victory Outreach. If the congregation is typical this Sunday morning, the congregation is young (under twenty-one), predominantly brown, predominantly male. Men wearing dark suits and ties sit poking their index fingers into the soft flanks of the Bibles they hold on their knees. The faces, the accents are Hispanic; the grammar is second-generation American; the liturgy borrows idioms from the American South. Here souls rap on the sweating skins of tambourines to be reborn.

A woman of about twenty-five smooths her skirt, squares her shoulders, stands to confess her travail.

The Catholic part of me—ancient, cynical, feminine—is appalled by the nakedness, the humorlessness, the sweetness of evangelical conversion narratives.

This is where it's at, man, the young woman sobs. Her eyes are sealed against the city. Tears commence. Her right hand is raised above her head.

I sit watching this woman's son, a boy of seven, watching his mother testify. This is what he knows. This is what he will grow to assume—to embrace or to reject. One generation and a four-hundred-year-old difference of opinion separate me from that boy.

■　■　■

The Latin American Novel

*On a weekday in summer, long ago, I am riding my bicycle
past the Fremont Presbyterian Church. The church door is open
so I stop to look. Painters on scaffolds are painting the walls white.
I walk in. The room glows with daylight drawn through yellow
glass windows. There are no side altars, no statues. There is a
wooden pulpit. And a table on which stands a plain wooden cross.
There are no kneelers in the pews. Don't Presbyterians pray on
their knees? This is only a room—a place of assembly—now empty
but for its honeyed light and its painters. Whereas my church is
never empty so long as the ruby burns in the sanctuary lamp, but
my church is filled with all times and all places. All the same, I
like this plain room, this empty Protestant shell. I ponder it as I
ride away. . . .*

■ ■ ■

An old nun, old and as white as a lizard, used to pray in Sacred
Heart Church when I was a boy. One day, as I passed her pillar,
her hand shot out to catch my sleeve; her regard shone on me in
the gloom. "If you are ever in church, and for one reason or
another you cannot pray," she whispered, "then ask God to unite
your lazy prayers to the good prayers of the people kneeling around
you."

Such was the lesson of my Catholic childhood. The prayerful
life of the Church is a communal achievement, prayer going on
like the tide of the sea. The implication of Catholicism is that
man is powerless alone. Catholicism is a religion of mediation.
The Church is our mother, because she serves as intermediary
between God, the God of the upraised hand, and men and women,
little two-legged mortals. Catholics are children.

Catholicism may be administered by embarrassed, celibate
men, but the intuition of Catholicism is voluptuous, feminine,
sure. The Church is our mother; the Church is our bride.

In its purest mold, Protestantism is male. Young men in Latin

America, young men in the Mission District of San Francisco, recoil from the skirts of Catholicism. They stand at the back of the church or they loiter outside. (Still Catholic enough to be confident, thereby, of their inclusion.) Catholicism would remind men that they are helpless; treats men like children. So men act like children. Whereas the call of evangelical Protestantism is a call to manhood, a call to responsibility.

A man with a diamond goatee and cut face stands before the Victory Outreach congregation:

I gang-banged, messed up, rolled queers. I've stuck the blade all the way in and felt a heart flutter like a pigeon on the end of my poker 'n' I felt no remorse.

UNTIL I FOUND JESUS CHRIST.

Diets and New Year's resolutions are Protestant things. Among Catholics there is often an amused condescension regarding converts who take religion too seriously, who are preoccupied with theology, who try to match the communal faith. You might as well try to match a spring day. Catholicism is just there, a way of life that need never come to a head. Catholicism never stands or falls on one decision. Catholicism isn't a novel.

The problem with Catholicism, the huge pillow-breasted consolation of Catholicism, is that it is all-embracing. Catholicism can as easily define a hemisphere as a neighborhood. But what does it mean that Brazil is the largest Catholic country in the world if nobody there goes to mass?

The Catholic Church assumes it is the nature of men and women to fail. You can be a sinner and remain a Catholic. You must consider yourself a sinner to remain a good Catholic. Bohemians and poets from Protestant climes gravitate toward the romance of Catholic countries or Catholic cities or Catholic parts of cities— wherever tragedy hangs its shingle; wherever tragedy holds sway.

Everyone knows that Catholics run better restaurants than Protestants.

Life is hard. Flesh is weak. Consolation is in order. Lapses are allowed for. Catholics have better architecture and sunnier plazas and an easier virtue and are warmer to the touch. At its best, Catholicism is all-forgiving.

Do not wonder that my Catholic aunts on the telephone are now discussing what they will wear to the Protestant wedding.

Protestants run cleaner police departments and courts of law than Catholics. Protestant trains smell better than Catholic trains and they run on time.

Four evangelical missionaries from southern California arrive in Guatemala. They have come over the mountain to convince Latin America of optimism. Their hair is slicked; they are pale as Pauline corpses; each carries a Bible. Never mind the Bible. Each wears a dark suit.

Tourists from the United States will still find much opportunity to be appalled by the accretion of beauty in Latin American churches; by the accretion of poverty in Latin American churches—peasants scraping their knees before statues. And the statues! Christ humiliated, a nest of thorns raking his brow.

Yes, yes, yes, chimes the Mexican priest. Christ was a loser. Catholicism is a religion for losers. The evangelical cannot account for failure. The evangelical turns his back on the cross. The evangelical refuses the entire wisdom of Latin America: Suffering is redemptive.

Two teenagers from Latin America tell me they converted to evangelical Protestantism because American Protestants came to their villages dressed in suits and ties. The evangelical appearance advertises an end to failure.

Suddenness is holy! For the young, who have no time to waste, the glamour of evangelical conversion—akin to barbells and eye shadow—is the promise of sudden change.

■ ■ ■

There is a crucifix over my bed. I am in bed; my eyes are open. I am waiting for the sound of midnight—a blare of horns, a fire whistle, a dog's bark, a woman's scream.

Larry Faherty is in New Orleans for Christmas, so we have not spent New Year's Eve together. He sent me a postcard, written in Spanish. It's there on my dresser.

A car passes on the wet pavement outside. My room revolves on a rail of light. And then it is dark. January 1, 1960. The new decade has come to Sacramento, California. It is no longer Christmas. In the morning there will be a cold mass at church, and then the Rose Parade on TV. And the long gray afternoon will pass away through a series of black-and-white football games; in a few days I will be back at school.

The ectoplasmic corpus of the crucifix glows with confidence. Awake on my bed, I am inclined forward: I want the years coming to improve me, to make my hand a man's hand and my soul a man's soul.

Every New Year's Eve my mother weeps in front of the TV when Guy Lombardo strikes up "Auld Lang Syne."

The crowd in Times Square cheers.

This year, however, we have gone to bed early. The back-porch light is on for my brother. I have stayed awake in the dark to feel the difference of a new decade.

There is no difference.

■ ■ ■

In the colored pages of *Life* magazine, the old dead pope with his purple face and his hooked nose is borne aloft through St. Peter's. The American experience of Catholicism as an immigrant faith, a ghetto contest of them against us, is coming to an end during my grammar-school years. My generation will be the last to be raised with so powerful a sense of the ghetto Church, so powerful a sense of the universal Church. An American of Irish descent and good looks will soon be elected president, our first Catholic president of the United States. As the old dead moth of a pope is swept under the doors of death, American Catholics are entering the gates of the city. A fat, expressive Italian pope will soon call his Church to *aggiornamento*, a rapprochement with the non-Catholic world.

For a time, the nuns will go on neatly dividing the world, as if they remain the Fates they have always been. We are the Catholics and all others, alas, are defined by the fact of their difference from us.

At Christian Brothers High School the governing ethos is tough, male. Because there is order in the cosmos, there will be order in the classroom—marches, genuflections, reverend address. I am indebted to my elders, the scholars, the theologians who preceded me. My teacher, by definition, assumes authority.

If you're so smart, Faherty, why come to school at all?

During a high-school religious retreat, the traveling Redemptorist (with a crucifix slung in his sash like a blunderbuss) brays counsel to an assembly of five hundred boys. There is the one about the boy who went away to a non-Catholic college and lost his faith because he was encouraged to think he could find all the answers by himself, fool. The sin of pride.

Pride is lonely, men, lonely as hell.

In 1961, in Brother Paul's French class, Larry Faherty drums his pencil eraser upon a closed French grammar. God, he is bored with Brother Paul, with French, with Sacramento.

Fuck French. Fuck Christian Brothers. Fuck Sacramento.

We are the odd couple. Larry is six feet tall, fair, Spanish-speaking. I answer in English. We take the Greyhound to San Francisco to eat Basque dinners. We would go anywhere to see *Black Orpheus*, our favorite movie. Larry tells me what I should have known about sex, about girls, letting his line down tenderly, a little at a time, into the clear pool of my imagination. Larry saw a man shot down to a pool of blood on a street in Mexico City. So, you see, he knows what life is. Larry is attractive to older girls.

On Friday nights, Larry honks for me in his father's Chrysler, the cigarette already dangling from his lip.

"Salutti Beulah Mumm," he calls out to the lighted window of Beulah Mumm, the librarian, who lives next door to us.

"There's something funny about that kid," my father says, as my father bends down to pick up the evening paper.

"Salutti Ferrucci," Larry honks at the house of Mrs. Ferrucci, at the end of the block.

We go to a jazz coffee house, The Bitter End. We order espressos. I never finish mine. Black musicians with preoccupied red eyes play for dulling hours. It amuses Larry to overtip the waitress—sometimes two or three times the amount of the bill—"to see what she will do." She keeps the money, of course, and with a poker face.

I won't hitchhike. I won't smoke cigarettes. I won't speak Spanish. I won't drink beer. And yet, I think, Larry senses Mexico in me. If I am his Negro, he is mine too. His casual relationship to money, his house with a swimming pool, these I take as ethnic traits. What he sees in me is innocence. He is all casualness about the things I intend to have. And I want what he claims to discard. I ingratiate myself with Larry Faherty's parents and I get invited down to southern California beach towns, where they spend the last weeks of August.

The Latin American Novel

One summer, Larry and I work together for the election of John F. Kennedy. My father says we are wasting our time—it will never happen. Larry is also selling magazine subscriptions, door to door. Larry's mother disapproves of this job. Larry works for a twenty-year-old man from Alabama.

Kennedy is elected.

The twenty-year-old runs off with Larry's paycheck.

Larry shrugs and tells me about the man's tattoos, all over his body, like some kind of lizard.

The swarming dots of the television screen begin to compose themselves into black faces during the nightly news. The civil-rights movement is gaining national attention. Black Protestantism has until now seemed to me a puzzling exhibition of perspiring women and wet-voiced men. Then the face of Dr. Martin Luther King, Jr., appears on the evening news and everything I think I know about saints begins to dissolve as I contemplate that face, as I listen to that voice. I begin to believe in heroes.

For two or three years Larry and I know each other better than we know anyone else in the world. When it is time to graduate, I aim for the rich man's college—"Stahn-ford," Larry says with a plummy cartoon voice, disapproving my choice.

By the time I get to Stanford, I believe in man-made history. I tutor ghetto children. I parade through downtown Palo Alto toward my first antiwar rally. All that stuff. I am an English major at Stanford; increasingly, though, I take courses in religion, mainly Protestantism. I still visit Brother Michael when I am home, but it is not the same. I choose a new hero—a Protestant theologian named Robert McAfee Brown. These are the years of ecumenism, and I have outgrown any caution regarding contact with non-Catholics. I eagerly bite into the Protestant apple the nuns had warned me against. I admit its sweetness.

By the next summer, I have new friends. I go to New York on

the Greyhound. I am invited into my first Park Avenue apartment.
I am interested in their sailcloth shirts and the brown slacks that
the mother wears without apology. The tinkle of ice cubes. The
books. They quarrel in front of me.

So begin my Protestant years. I am attracted to the modesty of
style, the unencumbered voices of Luther and Calvin and Park
Avenue—free—free of the trinketed cynicism of Mexico and the
nagging poetry of Ireland. I feel a masculine call to action. One
week, Dr. McAfee Brown is flying to Rome to serve as an official
Protestant delegate to the Vatican Council. All the while he is
writing books; he knows more about Catholicism than the nuns
could have told me. The next week, he will be off to Selma.

Larry Faherty is off at college, too—Boony U., he calls it.
There is some kind of trouble. (Larry is vague on the phone.) He
transfers to another college in the Midwest. We exchange letters.
We see each other at Christmas. He is becoming sadder, handsome.

By the end of the decade, I will be enrolled at Columbia
University, in a religious-studies program. I will take most of my
courses across the street at Union Theological Seminary.

Larry Faherty joins the Peace Corps, a fine young Kennedy
cadet. There is a war in Vietnam. Larry writes from Africa. Then
there is trouble again. Larry has been kicked out of the Peace
Corps "for not wearing pajamas," Larry is quoted as saying in
the Sacramento papers, which headline the story. A Peace Corps
official is vague in response.

Nineteen sixty-eight. We are, both of us, deep in the sixties
now. But Larry Faherty has nowhere to go once the sixties become
the Sixties. From Africa he quotes Ayn Rand; he grumbles about
the uniform answers of the fashionable left. Middle-class college
students reading *The Student as Nigger* put Larry in mind of the
rah-rah twits in a Wodehouse comedy. But his mood passes. His

liberal heart cannot justify America's war in Vietnam, and his next letter says so.

The letters become less frequent. I am living in New York. I hear he is living in Paris. I have no address for him there. In New York, at Columbia, student demonstrations in April close down the university. Politically, I still think of myself as of the left. I write letters to congressmen. I march in antiwar demonstrations up Fifth Avenue. But I cannot follow the decade all the way down the line. Date my defection from the murder of Dr. Martin Luther King, Jr. After his death, the Pauline vision of a society united is undermined by hack radicals like Stokely Carmichael, proclaiming a conventional protestant separatist line.

A manufactured sign in somebody's dormitory window urges passersby to QUESTION AUTHORITY.

Why—me with my Samsonite briefcase—why should one simply, as a matter of reflex, question authority? I continue to my carrel at the seminary library to confront the Protestant Reformation.

I read Puritan autobiographies, books of people who learned to read late in their lives. They speak from their pine houses and from within the rings of their candles about personal confrontations with God.

Were these the renowned, dour Puritans? Here, rather, were people who would not trust anyone over thirty.

The decade, alternately violent and sentimental, seems to me now a Protestant flowering. The famous activists of the 1960s were secular Jews who heralded a messianic future. But the true fathers of Woodstock, of sit-ins, and of rock pastoral were the dark-robed Puritan fathers.

An august cultural historian at Columbia University lectures on Galileo—the inevitable example—as I sit in the classroom and I am silent, though I would protest to him, if I were truly a protestant, that if the Church was wrong it may have been wrong for a valid reason. The Church sought to protect the communal vision, the Catholic world—a rounded, weighted, lovely thing—against an anarchy implicit in the admission of novelty. Novelty should only come from within the Church; a question not of facts but of authority.

How much can America hear from a Catholic schoolboy who defends the medieval Catholic dream? And how should I protest? Of what value to America are notions of authority, communality, continuity?

■ ■ ■

Dearest Ma,

I think this will not reach you till after the new year. By then I don't know where I'll be. What a lot I saw and what I have yet to see—Connemara and all the light of day sinking below the tide and my heart sank too. But there really is a new world, Ma, and it was already wearing my heart when I saw it, rising from the sea. New York City is hot as blazes and I'm looking down on a street so chock with dagos and Hebrews, so tattered and tangled and fast, it reminds me of the Italian scene on your second-best biscuit tin. Don't worry, Ma, there's a church not three streets away. I can count the bells from here. . . .

■ ■ ■

In the nineteenth century, Americans feared Jews as they feared Catholics, both tribes suspected of international allegiance. Jewish immigrants gloried in the country that honored separateness. Catholics, on the other hand, brought with them a sense of the necessity of the plural, and that sense was the best we gave in support of individualistic America.

In the 1840s, the nativist argument against allowing too many Irish into the U.S. pointed at Mexico. The United States would soon be at war with Mexico. The nativist fear was that the Irish would conspire with their fellow Catholics against the Protestant state.

It didn't happen. After the pneumatic hinge of the classroom door closed against Larry Faherty, all those years ago, a disproportionate number of those of us who remained inside Brother Michael's classroom would become policemen and judges and district attorneys and football coaches. There will be order in the cosmos because there is order in the classroom.

An Irish kid named Danny, who sits in front of me in Brother Paul's French class, and who this morning wears a red plaid shirt, will become a policeman. He will be driving down a rainy street and he will be killed by a rifle shot through the passenger window. A sergeant tenor will sing "Danny Boy" over the closed casket.

Ireland! I cannot imagine American Catholicism apart from the Irish. The Irish made themselves the advertisement for America—the most American of Catholics—while yet remaining the most Catholic of Americans.

Ireland told non-Catholic America all about us. The bow-tied Jewish raconteur and the bow-tied Irish raconteur took turns working the American psyche on *The Ed Sullivan Show*. You'd have thought there were only two brands of baloney in America. The Irishman told jokes about the Knights of Columbus and my parents laughed in recognition.

Every year the Irish strode up Fifth Avenue, craning their necks at all that WASP America held in trust for itself. I saw my first St. Patrick's Day parade from the windows of the University Club on Fifth Avenue. All afternoon I watched the Catholic centuries—the Puerto Ricans, the Hungarians, the Italians, the Portuguese—parade up the street of Rockefellers in the uniforms of Catholic high-school bands. For one symbolic day, the Irish accomplished the Catholic conversion of Protestant America by the merest insistence on the wearin' o' the green.

I saw Bobby Kennedy wave to the crowd.

Boatloads of young Irishmen arrived in the United States in the 1840s. Some ended up in the U.S. Army. Some ended up fighting in the war against Mexico.

The story has never been clear. Maybe something to do with the way the Americans behaved in Mexico. Perhaps it was the desecration of Mexican churches by U.S. soldiers, or perhaps the Irish recruits recalled Mother Ireland as they steeped themselves in the brothels of Mexico.

A small band of Irishmen did change sides during the Mexican-American War. In Mexico these Irishmen, San Patricios, are remembered as heroes—the St. Patrick's Brigade.

Despite the quantities of novels I have read, I find I do not believe in sudden shifts, revolutions of plot, reformations. My friendship with Larry Faherty has no denouement.

There is a vacuity, an abeyance, an alignment to the spring afternoon as I walk toward the Protestant seminary library, between mobs of jeering students, ranks of silent policemen.

My Puritan voices speak to me from their pine houses and from within the rings of their candles and I am moved by such solitary voices, their souls writing to mine, promising comfort, sharing a burden of loneliness. They were optimists, these haters of plays and of feasting, so different from my father's Latin skepticism and my mother's famous intimacy with the Virgin Mary, and even from this—Union Theological Seminary—the coldest, loneliest place I have ever been. Can one be born again? Can sin be overturned like a wooden bucket?

Rocks and bottles are thrown and horses charge in my wake.

Many of the hundreds of riot policemen on campus at Columbia that spring ate in the student cafeteria in John Jay Hall. They sat on one side of the cafeteria; most of the students sat on the other. I made a practice, a theatrical point, of sitting on the blue side, among what Catholic intuition taught me to recognize as the side of the angels. In the overarching debate I sought the Catholic side. The era's individualism seemed to me to stray too far from the communal need, an exploration of limits I privately called by its Catholic name: sin.

Something is now clear to me about Larry Faherty and that is my betrayal of him. The last time I saw Larry, he was ducking down in the back seat of my father's DeSoto in the parking lot of a Greyhound bus station. Larry had wanted to see me; sent word. Our meeting was rushed and lacked the fervor our past demanded. Larry was on the lam. He wasn't supposed to be in the country—"big trouble with Sam"—flicking his ash out the car window.

The driver of the Greyhound stood at the door of the bus. Passengers lined up, tossing away empty potato-chip bags and lighted cigarettes. The driver climbed back into his bucket seat. The engine chugged over.

"Salutti Beulah Mumm . . . ?"

Larry tried this on, pathetically recalling our intimacy, as he hoisted the duffel bag onto his shoulder. Just go, I thought to myself.

Then the pneumatic door sighed and swung to, sealing my blessed hero away. The last I heard, he was in Mexico, where I pray his rebellious soul is lapped by corrupt, warm waters.

The leader of the San Patricios, a rake named John Riley, eluded capture. The Irishmen who were apprehended by American forces were hanged as traitors by the U.S. Army one afternoon on the *zócalo* of Mexico City.

In 1973, I went to England to pursue a study of Puritanism and the rise of the novel. In London I sat late in the darkening library of the Warburg Institute, reading *Paradise Lost*. I became fascinated with the glamour of Milton's Satan, his iridescent tattoos. Then I was recalled by the Catholic necessity to avert my soul's eye from a Protestant logic that would make mere individualism a virtue.

■ ■ ■

I am introduced to a roomful of Catholic priests by the priest who calls himself Bill.

Hi, Bill.

Bill needed a speaker on "multiculturalism" for a retreat for new pastors. Someone in the Chancery Office gave Bill my name.

Multiculturalism: Catholic churches in California are crowding with Asian and Hispanic parishioners. In the Central Valley, the old families, the Italians and the Portuguese, grumble about the proliferation of Spanish masses and the Mexican takeover of parish festivals. In San Jose, the Vietnamese want their own masses, even their own priests.

There are twenty-five men in this room. Only one wears a Roman collar. If this priesthood is typical, it is predominantly white, predominantly middle-aged. (Hispanic priests have asked for and been granted permission to speak Spanish among themselves in the intervals between sessions.) The room looks like the dining room of a Ramada Inn. The view from the windows is of the brown hills above Danville, about twenty miles from San Francisco.

My Catholic schooling attempted to prepare me for many eventualities—for sex, for death—even to the loss of my faith. But I am not prepared to watch the Catholic Church stumble over a Protestant issue like multiculturalism.

No prayer begins our meeting.

When Catholic immigrants came to America in the nineteenth century, they proceeded according to the Catholic impulse, which was to hold on to the past. Nineteenth-century American Catholics constructed "national churches"—the German, the Polish, the

Lithuanian. What those Catholics seemed not to realize was that, in America, the Catholic impulse to preserve becomes the shortest path toward an American separatist faith.

In the last twenty years, the Church has again unwittingly chosen the path of ethnic separation. If, in California parishes, the majority of Catholics speak Spanish, then the Church speaks Spanish. But such pragmatism has divided congregations. When the nine-thirty mass is in English and the eleven o'clock mass is in Spanish, then what you've got is two separate parishes.

In one small Valley town I attended a "bilingual mass" at a church that is now third-generation Italian, newly Mexican. The priest rehearsed the liturgy line by line, first Spanish, then English; pretty smooth. The problem became apparent only with song. The Spanish hymns swelled the church, seemed to recall a Catholic world. When it came time to sing the English hymns—there were a couple of those—the church dwindled to the wheeze of an organ and two or three voices tottering like cups on saucers. Some Mexican kids snickered as the old white ladies sang their "Hail Holy Queen."

One priest raises his hand. Blue sweater. Mexican face. Contempt constraining his smile. "I have grandparents in my parish who want to pray with their grandchildren. What would you suggest?"

I suggest you have masses in Latin.

(Groans throughout the room. Blue Sweater half-turns in his chair to roll his eyes.)

Fine, I say (Asshole), *have your Spanish masses and your Vietnamese masses. But realize the Church is setting itself against inevitability; the inevitable Americanization of the grandchildren. You are going to lose the grandchildren; in fact, you've lost them already. You are papering your churches with poverty. You are using the poor to distract you from your failing enterprise. I'm beginning to suspect that you speak Spanish because in English you no longer believe. You are not feeding your lambs with Catholic assurances, you are feeding yourselves on the faith of immigrants. While second- and third-generation American Catholics go starving. A foreign-language liturgy should be a mere strategy, a temporary appeasement that should not distract us from our goal— the Catholic knowledge of union, the mystical body of Christ. We are Catholics, Fathers. We are Catholics living in America. But we are Catholics.*

I feel myself the only Catholic in this room.

No, that's not true. I understand these men well enough. I am their creation and they are mine. I still go to mass each Sunday. I go to a half-empty church. I go early—a "quiet mass," a low mass, a cold mass—so as not to dispel the illusion that the fat, full life of the Church is going on elsewhere, regardless, like the tide of the sea. . . .

What a pious, odd teenager I was. I made Larry Faherty leave the Tower Theater in the middle of *Elmer Gantry* because my soul felt kind of funny.

"Oh Jesus," Larry said, "now what?" But he was amused. . . .

A hand from the back. "So, what's your agenda?"

. . . And yet I was fascinated by the revival tent Protestantism the movie portrayed. When Larry and I went to San Francisco, we used to hang around Union Square after the bookstores, before the matinee, listening to evangelical preachers haranguing the lunchtime crowd. Larry loved Okie evangelists. He'd go up and get their pamphlets, sit smoking, chuckling to himself.

One Saturday, Larry and I were rewarded. A woman in a red coat parted the crowd with her elbows, knelt before the preacher, pleaded for conversion. The preacher stepped backward, aghast at his miracle. I thought of the cow giving birth to the calf at the State Fair. . . .

I have no agenda, Father. I am not a priest. I have no prescription, I have no intention. I am lonely. I tell you I see the disintegration of Catholicism in America and I tell you the Catholic Church does not attend to the paradox of American Catholic lives. We confess a communal faith; we live in an individualistic culture.

Look, here we are—Catholics—arguing about multiculturalism while secular America and even evangelical Protestantism take lessons from our tradition. Environmentalists, for example, question the wisdom of unbridled individualism. Environmentalists proclaim the enlightened imperative of a We. As Latin America turns Protestant, North America experiences the dawning of a Catholic vision—"the global village"—an ecology closer to medievalism than to the Industrial Age.

And now the United States is being evangelized by Latin Americans who have themselves been evangelized by the Protestant North. What do you make of that? Do you know what Latin Americans are saying about you? About us? They say the United States is such a sad place. So much tragedy! Latin America sees its mission in you. God so loves the United States that he has sent Latin America to save you. Victory Outreach has even begun sending missionaries to Paris. . . .

Good luck, says one of the priests. The others laugh.

Good News, rather. The other day I was jogging up the street past the Filipino evangelical church in my neighborhood. Every day they come from other parts of the city, pissing off the neighborhood by taking up all the parking places. They have predawn services, and evening prayer services, and they are in church on Sundays from dawn till dark. (This, while Catholic bishops sit in a closed circle discarding holy days.) (This, while my neighbors

*form a coalition seeking a court injunction against prayer services
after 7:00 P.M. so they can park their Land Rovers.) As I say, the
other day the Filipinos were swarming on the sidewalk and I was
forced to jog around them onto the street. I, too, dislike them—
their vans that go tweet-tweet when they back up and the little
dangling lucky things in the windows, yes, and I resent their
apostasy—how can they turn their backs on the faith of their
fathers? Yet, Fathers, how much they remind me of Catholics of
the fifties, and of the prayer life of the Church which seemed eternal
and ordinary.*

*For all of their obvious differences from Catholicism, I sense
among evangelicals a longing for some lost Catholic village, some
relief from loneliness. Perhaps this is inherent in all Protestantism;
the reason why Protestants enjoy such intensely communal worship.*

*Deep-dish Protestantism, beamed in a straight line from North
Carolina to Guatemala City, offers a tidy faith, the old way, rural
and close, albeit without the sentient authority of velvet and roses.
The small Protestant church revives the Catholic memory of the
countryside. In the small evangelical church, people who are demoralized by the city turn to the assurance of community. In the
small church, each soul has a first name again. One hand grips
another's hand against anonymity. Hymns resound over the city,
wild with grace, and the world becomes certain and small. . . .*

This room is large and silent and cold. The priests sit facing
me, their arms folded over their stomachs. These are the men
I wanted to become. My hand a man's hand. My soul a man's
soul . . .

Larry Faherty would roll his eyes at that one. Good old Larry.
At the State Fair I refused to eat the pork sandwich he bought
me at the Baptist booth. "It's okay, it's okay, it's not a sin,
goddammit, everything doesn't have to be a sin, Tonto."

"Phone the priest, then," I commanded.

He did, too. He found a telephone booth and he called a pastor somewhere—Larry said he could hear *Gunsmoke* in the background—who gave his permission to eat pork from a Baptist booth.

If it's the only sustenance available, son (Larry mimicked the brogue, passing the sandwich under my nose).

It was what I loved in Larry, his forgiveness of me. His forgiveness of all. His Catholicism. He smiled with pleasure as I bit into the Baptist sandwich; he laughed outright when gravy squirted onto my T-shirt. Then, all that evening, Larry deliberated the gravy stain, bending over to peer at it, stroking his imaginary beard: Hmmm . . . Mortal Sin/ Indelible Stain. Indelible Stain . . . (cradling his face in his hands, his eyes wildly rolling in their sockets) . . . MORTAL SIN!

My eyes move slowly around the room.

What happened to Brother Michael? I wrote to him. He never wrote back. That's what happened to Brother Michael. What happened to all of you? The Order of Melchizedek in rayon polo shirts, lending each other self-help books while American Catholics flock to AA meetings or Bly scout meetings or I-own-my-own-body meetings or yuppie reading groups where the more *challenging* Latin American novels are explored. . . .

The sin of pride, Rodriguez.

When I was a boy, an old nun used to pray in Sacred Heart Church. One day the old nun leaned over and whispered to me, If you are over in church and find yourself unable to pray. . . .

■   ■   ■

Turn to page 454. Line 137.

. . . brilliant Achilleus held the head
sorrowing, for this was his true friend he escorted toward
Hades. . . .

And now brilliant swift-footed Achilleus remembered one more thing.

He stood apart from the pyre and cut off a lock of fair hair which he had grown long to give to the river Spercheios, and gazing in deep distress out over the wine-blue water, he spoke forth:

SALUTTI BEULAH MUMM!

CHAPTER TEN

Nothing Lasts
a Hundred Years

A waiter bowed. The dining room was flooded with sunlight. I saw my mother sitting alone at a table near the window.

Where's Papa?

I turned to see my father enter the dining room. His hand moved to adjust his tie. Some pleasure tempted his lips.

He had gotten up early. He had taken a walk. He had gone to the Capuchin church on the Via Veneto. I remembered the church—the monk murmuring at the drop of a coin—and, several flights down, I remembered the harvest of skulls.

For years I had dreamed of this trip with my parents. We were many years from Sacramento. We were in Rome at the Eden Hotel. This was to have been my majority the grand tour proof of my sophistication, my easy way with the world. This was to have been the culmination of our lives together, a kind of antiheaven. My father should have been impressed.

But nothing I could show my father, no Michelangelo, no Bernini, no cathedral or fountain or square, would so rekindle an enthusiasm in my father's eyes as that paltry catacomb he had

found on his own. He had seen the final things. He was confirmed
in his estimate of nature. He was satisfied.

．　．　．

I was born in the year 1632, in the city of York, of a good
family, though not of that country, my father being a foreigner
of Bremen. . . . I was called Robinson Kreutznaer; but by the
usual corruption of words in England we are now called, nay,
we call ourselves, and write our name 'Crusoe' . . .

Being the third son of the family, and not bred to any
trade, my head began to be filled very early with rambling
thoughts. . . . My father, a wise and grave man, gave me
serious and excellent counsel against what he foresaw was
my design.

When I was fourteen and my father was fifty, we toyed with
the argument that had once torn Europe, South from North, Catholic from Protestant, as we polished the blue DeSoto.

"Life is harder than you think, boy."

"You're thinking of Mexico, Papa."

"You'll see."

．　．　．

We arrived late on a summer afternoon in an old black car. The
streets were arcades of elm trees. The houses were white. The
horizon was flat.

Sacramento, California, lies on a map around five hundred
miles from the ruffled skirt of Mexico. Growing up in Sacramento,
I found the distance between the two countries to be farther than
any map could account for. But the distance was proximate also,
like the masks of comedy and tragedy painted over the screen at
the Alhambra Theater.

Both of my parents came from Mexican villages where the bells
rang within an hour of the clocks of California. I was born in San
Francisco, the third of four children.

When my older brother developed asthma, the doctors advised

a drier climate. We moved one hundred miles inland to Sacramento.

Sacramento was a ladies' town—"the Camellia Capital of the World." Old ladies in summer dresses ruled the sidewalks. Nature was rendered in Sacramento, as in a recipe, through screens—screens on the windows; screens on all the doors. My mother would close the windows and pull down the shades on the west side of the house "to keep out the heat" through the long afternoons.

My father hated Sacramento. He liked an open window. When my father moved away from the ocean, he lost the hearing in one ear.

Soon my mother's camellias grew as fat and as waxy as the others on that street. She twisted the pink blossoms from their stems to float them in shallow bowls.

Because of my mother there is movement, there is change in my life. Within ten years of our arrival in Sacramento, we would leap from one sociological chart onto another, and from house to house to house—each house larger than the one before—all of them on the east side of town. By the time I went to high school, we lived on "Eye" Street, in a two-story house. We had two cars and a combination Silvertone stereo-television. My bedroom was up in the trees.

I am not unconscious. I cherish our fabulous mythology. My father makes false teeth. My father received three years of a Mexican grammar-school education. My mother has an American high-school diploma. My mother types eighty words per minute. My mother works in the governor's office, where the walls are green. Edmund G. "Pat" Brown is governor. Famous people walk by my mother's desk. Chief Justice Earl Warren says hi to my mother.

After mass on Sundays, my mother comes home, steps out of

her high-heel shoes, opens the hatch of the mahogany stereo, threads three Mexican records onto the spindle. By the time the needle sinks into the artery of memory, my mother has already unwrapped the roast and is clattering her pans and dinking her bowls in the kitchen.

It was always a man's voice. Mexico pleaded with my mother. He wanted her back. Mexico swore he could not live without her. Mexico cried like a woman. Mexico raged like a bull. He would cut her throat. He would die if she didn't come back.

My mother hummed a little as she stirred her yellow cake.

My father paid no attention to the music on the phonograph. He was turning to stone. He was going deaf.

I am trying to think of something my father enjoyed.

Sweets.

Any kind of sweets. Candies. Nuts. Especially the gore oozing from the baker's wreath. Carlyle writes in *The French Revolution* about the predilection of the human race for sweets; that so much of life is unhappiness and tragedy. Is it any wonder that we crave sweets? Just so did my father, who made false teeth, love sweets. Just so does my father, to this day, disregard warnings on labels. Cancer. Cholesterol. As though death were the thing most to be feared in life.

My mother remembered death as a girl. When a girl of my mother's village died, they dressed the dead girl in a communion dress and laid her on a high bed. My mother was made to look; whether my mother was made to kiss that cold girl I do not know, but probably she did kiss her, for my mother remembered the scene as a smell of milk.

My mother would never look again. To this day, whenever we go to a funeral, my mother kneels at the back of the church.

But Mexico drew near. Strangers, getting out of dusty cars, hitching up their pants, smoothing their skirts, turned out to be relatives, kissing me on the front porch. Coming out of nowhere—full-blown lives—staying a month (I couldn't remember our lives before they came), then disappearing when back-to-school ads began to appear in the evening paper.

Only my Aunt Luna, my mother's older sister, lives in Sacramento. Aunt Luna is married to my uncle from India, his name an incantation: Raja Raman. We call him Raj. My uncle and aunt came to the Valley before us. Raj is a dentist and he finds work where he can, driving out on weekends to those airless quonset-hut villages where farmworkers live. His patients are men like himself—dark men from far countries—men from India, from Mexico, from the Philippines.

One Sunday in summer my father and I went with my Uncle Raj and my Aunt Luna to Lodi, about thirty miles south of Sacramento. There was a brown lake in the center of Lodi where blond teenagers skied. We stopped to eat lunch in the shade of a tree and then we drove on, past dust-covered vineyards.

We stopped at an old house. I remember the look on my Aunt Luna's face. My father and my uncle got out of the car. There was some question about whether or not I should go with them. Aunt Luna fretted. "Don't be afraid of anything you'll see," she said. "It's just an old house where some men live." Aunt Luna stayed in the car.

Inside, the house is dark. The front-room windows are painted over. There are cots along the walls. On several cots men recline. They are dressed. Are they sick? They watch as we pass. We hear only the sound of our steps on the boards of the floor.

A crack of light shines from behind a door at the rear of the house. My uncle pushes open the door. A man wearing an apron is stirring a pot.

Romesh!

Romesh quickly covers the pot. He kisses my uncle on the

mouth. He shakes hands with my father. Then, turning to me, he salutes: "General."

Romesh was Raj's older brother. Every Christmas, when Romesh came to my uncle's house, he called me the general. My brother was the colonel. Romesh came with his sister—"the doctor." One time he stood on his head. Every Christmas, Romesh and his sister gave me presents that either had no sex or should have gone to a girl. Once, a green cup; another year, a string of pearls. I was never sure if there was menace in Romesh.

Uncle Raj offered my father a job managing a "boardinghouse"—like the one in Lodi—where derelicts slept.

In private my mother said no, Leo, no.

My father ended up working in the back room of my uncle's office on J Street, making false teeth for several dentists. My father and Uncle Raj became closest friends.

My classmates at Sacred Heart School, two blocks from our house, belong to families with names that come from Italy and Portugal and Germany. We carry aluminum lunch boxes decorated with scenes from the lives of Hopalong Cassidy and Roy Rogers. We are an American classroom. And yet we are a dominion of Ireland, the Emerald Isle, the darling land. "Our lovely Ireland," the nuns always call her.

During the hot Sacramento summers, I passed afternoons in the long reading gallery of nineteenth-century English fiction. I took an impression of London and of the English landscape. Ireland held no comparable place in my literary imagination. But from its influence on my life I should have imagined Ireland to be much larger than its picayune place on the map. As a Catholic schoolboy I learned to put on the brogue in order to tell Catholic jokes, of grave diggers and drunkards and priests. Ireland sprang from the tongue. Ireland set the towering stalks of the litanies of the Church to clanging by its inflection. Ireland was droll. Ireland was omniscient, Ireland seeping through the screen of the confessional box.

And did your mother come from Ireland? Around March 17, a Catholic holiday, my Mexican mother—that free-floating patriot —my mother begins to bristle a bit. "If it's so wonderful, why did they all leave?" But it is her joke sometimes, too, that we are Irish. My mother's surname is Moran, her father a black Irishman? Her father was tall with eyes as green as leaves. There were Irish in nineteenth-century Mexico, my mother says. But there is no family tree to blow one way or the other. The other way would lead to Spain. For Moran is a common enough name in Spain, as throughout Latin America. Could it have been taken, not from Ireland but to Ireland, by Spaniards—Spanish sailors shipwrecked by Elizabeth's navy?

When my younger sister asked me to help her with an essay for school (the topic was Ireland), I dictated a mouthful of clover about Dublin's Jewish mayor and Ed Sullivan, Dennis Day, Mayor Daley, Carmel Quinn. "Ireland, mother of us all. . . ."

The essay won for my sister an award from the local Hibernian society. I taunted my sister the night she had to dress up for the awards banquet. My mother, though, returned from the banquet full of humor. They had all trooped into the hall behind the Irish colors—my sister, my mother, my father, an assortment of ladies, and some white-haired priests.

When Father O'Neil came back from his first trip home to Ireland, I was in third grade. There was a general assembly at school so we could see his slides, rectangles of an impossible green bisected by a plane's wing. The relations lined up in front of white houses, waving to us or just standing there. There was something so sad about Father then, behind the cone of light from the projector, in Sacramento, at Sacred Heart School, so far from the faces of home and those faces so sad.

Days of Obligation

Ireland was where old priests returned to live with their widowed sisters and (one never said it) to die. So it was a big white cake and off you go. Ireland was our heart's home. I imagined the place from St. Patrick's Day cards—a cottage, a bell on the breeze, the breeze at my back, through quilted meadows and over the winding road.

Sacramento, my Sacramento, then, must seem to Father O'Neil as flat and as far away as Africa in the Maryknoll missionary movies. Life was the journey far from home, or so I decided as I watched Father O'Neil popping squares of memory upside down into a projector.

My mother remembered a train ride across the Mexican desert. Her brother, her only, her darling Juan, had come to California to find work. When he earned money enough he sent for his widowed mother and his five sisters. My mother was eight years old when she left Mexico. Poking her head out of the carriage window, she got cinders in her hair, which made her sisters laugh.

On that same train were nuns disguised in cotton dresses. They wore hats and gloves. The nuns were fleeing religious persecution in Mexico. An Irish pastor had promised them a convent in California. My mother sang for them.

In my own version of my life, I was not yet the hero—perhaps California was the hero, perhaps my mother. I used to lie awake in the dark and imagine myself on a train far, far away, hurtling toward the present age of my parents. Forty-six. Forty-six. I used to imagine my future as the story of the Welsh coal miner's son who leaves home to take the high road to London. But, as it was, I didn't come from Ireland or India. I was born at the destination.

In the 1950s, billboards appeared on the horizon that beckoned restless Americans toward California. Sacramento of the 1950s was the end of the Middle Ages and Sacramento growing was the beginning of London.

Nothing Lasts a Hundred Years

In those days, people were leaving their villages and their mothers' maiden names to live among strangers in tract houses and God spoke to each ambition through the GI Bill. Highways swelled into freeways. If you asked, people in Sacramento said they were from Arkansas or from Portugal. Somewhere else.

■ ■ ■

It was my father who told me that an explorer with my surname, Juan Rodríguez Cabrillo, had been the first European to see California, rising and falling on the sea. The Irish nun at school confirmed the sighting. California was the farthest outpost of the Spanish colonial empire, Sister said. "Mexico City was the capital of the New World."

Mexico was the old country. In the basement of my Aunt Luna's house, I'd seen the fifty-gallon drums destined for Mexico, drums filled with blankets, flannel shirts, wrinkled dresses, faded curtains. When things got old enough they went to Mexico, where the earth shook and buildings fell down and old people waited patiently amid the rubble for their new old clothes.

I was repelled by Mexico's association with the old. On the map in Sister Mary Regis's classroom, Mexico was designated OLD MEXICO. In my imagination, Mexico was a bewhiskered hag huddled upon an expanse of rumpled canvas that bore her legend: Old Mexico.

Mexico City had universities and printing presses, cathedrals, palanquins, periwigs, long before there were British colonies in New England, Sister said. Long before there were cathedrals in Mexico, or periwigs or palanquins, there had been Indians in California. They had long hair. They wore no clothes. They ate acorns. They moved camp often. The fifth-grade textbook couldn't remember much else about them. (They looked like me.)

Alongside the duck pond at Sutter's Fort was a replica of an

Indian teepee, but the wrong kind—a Plains Indian teepee—a tripod covered with painted leather.

Tall silvery grasses were bound into sheaflike water boats. California Indians paddled up and down the watery marshes of the Central Valley, which at that time looked very much like a duck-hunting print, said Sister, holding one up: a wedge of ducks driven into a rosy dawn.

In the nineteenth century, an unnamed Spanish explorer had come over the foothills from San Francisco Bay. The unnamed explorer nevertheless brought names; he flung names like blue-rocks; he consigned names to every creek and river. He named the valley Sacramento to honor the sacramental transformation of bread and wine into the body and blood of Christ. The river, which Californians would later call the Sacramento, the explorer named Jesús María. There were saints' names and Mary's name all up and down California.

In the 1950s, it seemed odd to me that non-Catholics went along with all this. They mispronounced the Spanish words, it's true. In Spanish, Sacramento gets a pinwheel in the middle—a twirling "r." Valley pronunciation flattened the word—trampled the "sack"—but then the Valley was flat. And Sacramento was a Protestant town.

My school was named to honor the Sacred Heart, which symbolized the ardor of Christ for His people—a heart with an open valve, spewing flame. Public schools in town were named to honor nineteenth-century American men, adventurers and civilizers, men crucial to the Protestant novel: Kit Carson, John Frémont, C. K. McClatchy, James Marshall. The most common naming name was that of John Sutter, Sacramento's founding father. Sutter's name attached to two hospitals in town; a boulevard; a men's club across from the state capitol; a public park; a tennis club.

Sutter's Fort was our historical landmark. Sutter's Fort was across the street from the new Stop'n'Shop, a ten-minute bicycle ride from my house. Sutter's Fort held no mystery for me. The grass was mowed once a week. The fort was surrounded on weekdays by yellow school buses. Not that Sacramento's memory of John Sutter was an unmixed pride. Sutter was a founding father notable for his failure. His story spelled a lesson in the Protestant annals.

Johann Sutter arrived in the 1830s, when California was Mexican territory. He had come from a low, delftish sky, from Bavaria, from Calvin, from Zwingli. When Sutter arrived in Monterey, he proposed to Mexican officials that he would build a fort in the great valley over the coastal hills. The fort would be a European settlement—New Helvetia he called it—a wall against the Indians. Mexico granted permission. Sutter paid no money to become a duke of wind and grass, the last European in a nineteenth-century opera.

As a young man, as a silent man, courting my mother, my father spent what little money he had on opera tickets, purchasing the extravagant gesture. When my father was seven years old, his mother died giving birth to a baby named Jesús. My father remembered lightning. How it rained that night! His father bundled up the blood-soaked sheets and the shift she wore, and with his son (my father carried the lantern), he went out into the storm to bury them. A few months later the baby died.

My father remembered the funeral of his father—the coffin floating on the shoulders of the men of the village, as if on a river, down the hill to the cemetery. As the casket was lowered into the pit, my father stepped forward to look down and he saw the bones of a hand reaching upward. My father never afterward passed up an opportunity to look into an open casket.

Infrequently, after dinner, my father told ghost stories.

"It doesn't happen here," my mother would say to her children, leaning into the story like an unwanted shaft of sunlight. "It happened in Mexico. Those things happen in old countries. During the Revolution, people used to bury their gold. When they died, they needed to come back to tell their children to dig up the money, so they could rest in peace. It doesn't happen here."

At the Saturday matinee at the Alhambra Theater we sat in the dark, beneath proximate grimaces of comedy and tragedy, laughing at death—we laughed at that pathetic tourist, the Creature from the Black Lagoon. For we were the sons and daughters of Arkies and Okies and the Isles of the Azores. Parents, grandparents—someone near enough to touch, someone close enough to whisper—had left tragedy behind. Our parents had crossed the American River, had come to Sacramento where death had no dominion. To anyone who looked back from the distance of California, the words of the dead were like mouths opening and closing in a silent film.

■ ■ ■

Sacramento's ceremonial entrance was the Tower Bridge, where a sign proclaimed the town's population as 139,000. From the bridge you could see the state capitol—a wedding cake topped by a golden dome. Then, for six blocks, Sacramento posted BAIL BONDS; WEEKLY RATES; JESUS SAVES. Skid Row was what remained of the nineteenth-century river town, the Sacramento one sees in the early lithographs—a view from the river in the 1850s: young trees curling upward like calligraphic plumes; wooden sidewalks; optimistic storefronts; saloons; hotels; the Eagle Theater.

In the 1950s, Sacramento had begun to turn away from the land. Men who "worked for the state" wore white short-sleeved shirts downtown. There were office buildings, hotels, senators. Sacramento seemed to me a long way from the Okie evangelists at the far end of the car radio. Except for Mexican farmworkers, I rarely saw men wearing cowboy hats downtown.

Nothing Lasts a Hundred Years

The urban progress of Sacramento in the 1950s—the pouring of cement and of asphalt—imitated, even as it attempted to check, the feared reclamation of California by nature. But in the 1950s there was plenty of nature left. On summer evenings, houses became intolerable. We lolled on blankets on the grass. We were that much closer to becoming Indians.

Summer days were long and warm and free and I could make of them what I liked. America rose, even as the grasses, even as the heat, even as planes rose. America opened like a sprinkler's fan, or like a book in summer. At Clunie Library the books which pleased me most were about boyhood and summer and America; synonyms.

I hate the summer of Sacramento. It is flat and it is dull. Though it is not yet noon, the dry heat of Sacramento promises to rise above the leaves to a hundred degrees. Just after noon, the California Zephyr cuts through town, pauses for five minutes, stopping traffic on K and L, and for those five minutes I inhabit the train's fabulous destination. But then the train sweeps aside like the curtain at the Memorial Auditorium, to reveal the familiar stage set for a rural comedy. A yellow train station.

Yet something about the Valley summer is elemental to me and I move easily through it—the cantaloupe-colored light, the puddles of shade on the street as I bicycle through. There is a scent of lawn.

When I think of Sacramento, I think of lawns—force-fed, prickling rectangles of green. Lawns are not natural to California. Even one season without water, without toil, is ruinous to a garden, everyone knows. The place that had been before—before California—would come back; a place the Indians would recognize. Lovely tall grasses of dandelion or mustard in spring would inevitably mean lapsarian weeds, tinder grass and puncture vines come summer.

213

On Saturdays I mow the front lawn. On my knees I trim the edges. Afterward I take off my shoes to water down the sidewalk. Around noontime, as I finish, the old ladies of Sacramento, who have powdered under their arms and tied on their summer straw hats, walk by and congratulate me for "keeping your house so pretty and clean. Whyn't you come over to my house now," the ladies say.

I smile because I know it matters to keep your lawn pretty and green. It mattered to me that my lawn was as nice as the other lawns on the block. Behind the American façade of our house, the problem was Ireland. The problem was India. The problem was Mexico.

Mexico orbited the memory of my family in bitter little globes of sorrow, rosary beads revolving through the crushing weight of my mother's fingers. Mexico. Mexico. My mother said Mexico had skyscrapers. "Do not judge Mexico by the poor people you see coming up to this country." Mexico had skyscrapers, pyramids, blonds.

Mexico is on the phone—long-distance.

Juanito murdered!

My mother shrieks, drops the phone in the dark. She cries for my father. For light.

A crow alights upon a humming wire, bobs up and down, needles the lice within his vest, surveys with clicking eyes the field, the cloud of mites, then dips into the milky air and flies away.

The earth quakes. The peso flies like chaff in the wind. The Mexican police chief purchases his mistress a mansion on the hill.

The doorbell rings.

I split the blinds to see three nuns standing on our front porch. Mama. Mama.

Nothing Lasts a Hundred Years

Monsignor Lyons has sent three Mexican nuns over to meet my parents. The nuns have come to Sacramento to beg for Mexico at the eleven o'clock mass. We are the one family in the parish that speaks Spanish. As they file into our living room, the nuns smell pure, not sweet, pure, like candles or like laundry.

The nun with a black mustache sighs at the end of each story the other two tell: Orphan. Leper. Crutch. One-eye. Casket.

¡Qué lástima!

"Someday you will go there," my mother would say. "Someday you'll go down and with all your education you will be 'Don Ricardo.' All the pretty girls will be after you." We would turn magically rich in Mexico—such was the rate of exchange—our fortune would be multiplied by nine, like a dog's age. We would be rich, we would be happy in Mexico.

■ ■ ■

Of Mexico my father remembered the draconian, the male face—the mustache parted over the false promises of the city.

"What is there to miss?" My father leaned over the map of Mexico I had unfolded on my desk.

"Tell me about the village."

"It's not on the map." His finger moved back and forth across the desert, effacing.

"Tell me names, Papa, your family."

He was an orphan in Mexico. My father had no private Mexico, no feminine corner. From the age of eight my father worked for rich relatives, a poor relation on the sufferance of his uncle. He remembers a cousin, a teenage girl, who went to bed when the sun went down and wept all night. And there were aunts, young aunts with their hair packed into gleaming loaves; old aunts whose hair had shriveled into dry little buns. My father appears in none of the family photographs he has kept in a cigar box in the closet.

The family was prominent, conservative, Catholic in the Days

215

of Wrath—years of anti-Catholic persecution in Mexico. My father saw a dead priest twirling from the branch of a tree. My father remembered a priest hiding in the attic of his uncle's house. My father heard crowds cheering as the haughty general approached. My father remembered people in the crowd asking one another which general was passing, which general had just passed.

The church was my father's home; both of his parents were in heaven; the horizon was my father's home. My father grew up near the sea and he dreamed of sailing away. One day he heard a sailor boast of Australia. My father decided to go there.

My father's hand rests upon the map, a solitary continent, veined, unmoored. His native village was near enough to the town of Colima so that at night, as a boy, he saw the new electric glow of Colima instead of the stars. Colima, the state capital, has grown very large (a star on the map); perhaps what had been my father's village is now only a suburb of Colima?

He shrugs.

My father made false teeth for Dr. Wang. Mrs. Wang was the receptionist. Mrs. Wang sat at a bare table in an empty room. An old Chinese man, Dr. Wang's father, climbed the stairs at intervals to berate his son and his son's wife in Chinese.

Because of my mother, we lived as Americans among the middle class. Because of my father, because of my uncle from India, we went to Chinese wedding receptions in vast basement restaurants downtown, near the Greyhound station. We sat with hundreds of people; we sat in back; we used forks. When the waiter unceremoniously plopped wobbly pink desserts in front of us, my mother pushed my plate away. "We'll finish at home."

My father and my uncle worked among outsiders. They knew a handsome black doctor who sat alone in his office on Skid Row, reading the newspaper in his chair like a barber.

Sacramento was filling with thousands of new people each

year—people fleeing the tanks of Hungary, people fleeing their fathers' debts or their fathers' ghosts or their fathers' eyes.

One of my aunts went back to Mexico to visit and she returned to tell my mother that the wooden step—the bottom step—of their old house near Guadalajara was still needing a nail. Thirty years later! They laughed.

My father said nothing. It was as close as he came to praising America.

We have just bought our secondhand but very beautiful blue DeSoto. "Nothing lasts a hundred years," my father says, regarding the blue DeSoto, as regarding all else. He says it all the time—his counsel. I will be sitting fat and comfortable in front of the TV, reading my *Time* magazine. My mother calls for me to take out the garbage. *Now!* My father looks over the edge of the newspaper and he says it: Nothing lasts a hundred years.

Holiday magazine published an essay about Sacramento by Joan Didion. The essay, an elegy for old Sacramento, was about ghostly ladies who perched on the veranda of the Senator Hotel and about their husbands, who owned the land and were selling the land. Joan Didion's Sacramento was nothing to do with me; families like mine meant the end of them. I so thoroughly missed the point of the essay as to be encouraged that a national magazine should notice my Sacramento.

Whenever Sacramento made it into the pages of *Time* magazine, I noticed the editors always affixed the explanatory *Calif.*, which I took as New York City's reminder. We were nothing. Still, that caliphate had already redeemed our lives. My mother, my father, they were different in California from what history had in store for them in Mexico. We breathed the air, we ate the cereal, we drank the soda, we swam in the pools.

My father was surprised by California and it interested him. It interested him that Sacramento was always repairing itself. A streetlight would burn out, a pothole would open in the asphalt, a tree limb would crack, and someone would come out from "the city" to fix it. The gringos were always ready to fix things, my father said.

In high school I worked as a delivery boy for Hobrecht Lighting Company. I delivered boxes of light fixtures to new homes on the north side of the river.

I remember standing outside a house near Auburn, waiting for the contractor to come with a key. I stood where the backyard would be. The March wind blew up from the fields and I regretted the loss of nature—the fields, the clear distance.

Yet California was elemental to me and I could no more regret California than I could regret myself. Not the dead California of Spaniards and forty-niners and Joan Didion's grandmother, but Kodachrome, CinemaScope, drive-in California—freeways and new cities, bright plastic pennants and spinning whirligigs announcing a subdivision of houses; hundreds of houses; houses where there used to be fields. A mall opened on Arden Way and we were first-nighters. I craved ALL-NEW and ALL-ELECTRIC, FREE MUGS, and KOOL INSIDE and DOUBLE GREEN STAMPS, NO MONEY DOWN, WHILE-U-WAIT, ALL YOU CAN EAT.

At a coffee shop—open 24 hours, 365 days a year—I approved the swipe of the waitress's rag which could erase history.

Through the years I was growing up there, Sacramento dreamed of its own redevelopment. Plans were proposed every few months to convert K Street downtown into a mall and to reclaim a section of Skid Row as "Old Town." The *Bee* published sketches of the carnival future—an expansive street scene of sidewalk cafés with banners and clouds and trees that were also clouds and elegant ladies with their purse arms extended, pausing on sidewalks that were made of glass.

A few years later, the future was built. Old Sacramento became a block of brick-front boutiques; some squat glass buildings were constructed on Capitol Avenue; and K Street, closed to traffic for several blocks, got a concrete fountain and some benches with winos asleep in the sun.

Never mind. Never mind that the future did not always meet America's dream of itself. I was born to America, to its Protestant faith in the future. I was going to be an architect and have a hand in building the city. There was only my father's smile that stood in my way.

It wasn't against me; his smile was loving. But the smile claimed knowledge. My father knew what most of the world knows by now—that tragedy wins; that talent is mockery. In the face of such knowledge, my father was mild and manly. If there is trouble, if there is a dead bird to pick up, or when the lady faints in church, you want my father around. When my mother wants water turned into wine, she nudges my father, for my father is holding up the world, such as it is.

My father remains Mexican in California. My father lives under the doctrine, under the very tree of Original Sin. Much in life is failure or compromise; like father, like son.

For several years in the 1950s, when one of my family makes a First Holy Communion, we all go to Sutter's Fort to have our pictures taken. John Sutter's wall against the Indians becomes a gauge for the living, a fixed mark for the progress of my mother's children. We stand in formal poses against the low white wall of the fort. One of my sisters wears a white dress and veil and a little coronet of seed pearls. Or, when it is a boy's turn, one of us wears a white shirt, white pants, and a red tie. We squint into the sun. My father is absent from all the photographs.

The Sacramento Valley was to have been John Sutter's Rhineland. He envisioned a town rising from his deed—a town he decided, after all, to name for himself—Sutterville. Sutter imagined himself inventing history. But in the Eastern cities of Boston and Philadelphia and New York, Americans were imagining symmetry. They were unrolling maps and fixing them with weights set down upon the Pacific Ocean. Newcomers—Americans— were arriving in Mexican territory.

Already there were cracks in the sidewalk where the roots of the elm tree pushed up.

My father smiled.

Ask me what it was like to have grown up a Mexican kid in Sacramento and I will think of my father's smile, its sweetness, its introspection, its weight of sobriety. Mexico was most powerfully my father's smile, and not, as you might otherwise imagine, not language, not pigment. My father's smile seemed older than anything around me. Older than Sutter's Fort.

■ ■ ■

Priests were optimists. They were builders and golfers, drinkers of Scotch. They bellowed their Latin. They drove fast in dark cars. They wore Hawaiian shirts to compensate for tragedy. Priests' boyhoods were spent in dark, polished seminaries, as lovelorn, as masculine as my father's Mexico. Priests wore skirts. Parishioners gave priests hand towels with crosses embroidered on, or pen sets with crosses for clips, or handkerchiefs with little crosses in the corners, or notepapers embossed with praying hands. Priests told jokes to cover the embarrassment of such gifts; priests told jokes to cover the embarrassment of collecting money; priests told jokes to cover the embarrassment of life, for priests had the power to forgive sins.

Nuns were pragmatists. They were embarrassed by nothing. The Sisters of Mercy taught me confidence. When I came to their classrooms, unable, unwilling to speak English, the nuns methodically elected me. They picked on me. They would not let me be but I must speak louder, Richard, and louder, Richard.

Nothing Lasts a Hundred Years

I think of those women now, towers, linen-draped silos, inclining this way and that, and only their faces showing; themselves country lasses, daughters of Ireland. They served as my link between Mexico and America, between my father's dark Latin skepticism and the naïve cherry tree of Protestant imagining.

The only exception to the rule of confidence at school came with religion class. At the start of each school day, after the "Morning Offering," after the Pledge of Allegiance to the Flag of the United States of America, our young hearts were plunged in the cold bath of Ireland. For fifty minutes, life turned salt, a vale of tears. Our gallery, our history, our geography, was Ireland. The story of man was the story of sin, which could not be overcome with any such thing as a Declaration of Independence. Earth was clocks and bottles and heavy weights. Earth was wheels and rattles and sighs and death. We all must die. Heaven was bliss eternal. Heaven was a reign of grace bursting over the high city and over the mansions of that city. Earth was Ireland and heaven was Ireland. The dagger in Mary's heart was pain for her Son's passion. The bleeding heart of Jesus was sorrow for man's sin. Christ had instituted a church—a priesthood, sacraments, the mass—and men required all the constant intercession of the saints and the special help of Mother Mary to keep the high road. All alone, man would wander and err, like pagan Caesar or like Henry VIII.

At nine-thirty, the subject changed. The class turned to exercises of worldly ambition—to spelling, reading, writing—in preparation for adulthood in comic America. The nuns never reconciled the faces of comedy and tragedy and they never saw the need.

"Remember the Alamo," children in Sacramento learned to say. Remembering what?

Parades up Broadway on the Fourth of July enlisted equestrian clubs of blond businessmen dressed in tight pants, as Spanish

221

dons, together with their señoritas, sidesaddle, on charming palominos. Men who had seen war in Asia and Europe, the woman who had lost her only true love—they waved to the crowd. The past was something that sparkled in the sun or the past was something preserved from the sun, like the adobe rooms at Sutter's Fort.

My father mutters about the intrigues of Masonic lodges in Mexico.

That's only Mexico, Papa.

Most boys my age in Sacramento are wearing coonskin caps when my father tells how America stole the Southwest from Mexico, how Americans died at the Alamo to make Texas a slave state.

The United States has a different version.

On Sunday nights, we gather around the TV to watch *The Ballad of Davy Crockett*. My father is interested at first. The Mexicans surrounding Walt Disney's Alamo are buffoons with white suspenders crossed over their bellies. My father returns to his newspaper.

■ ■ ■

At noontime exactly on a clear winter day, California will officially become the largest, by which we mean the most populous, state in the union. Governor Edmund G. "Pat" Brown wants fire sirens and factory whistles; he wants honking horns and church bells to detonate the hour of our numerical celebrity. The bureaucrat's triumphant tally will change California forever.

Sacred Heart Church in Sacramento has no bells, none that ring, nothing to hang in this clear blue sky. There is a brick tower, a campanile, a shaft of air. When the church was built, neighbors had complained first thing about bells. So no bells ever rang at Sacred Heart.

Five to twelve: The Irish nun stands at her blackboard. Tat.

222

Nothing Lasts a Hundred Years

Tat. Tat. Slice. Tat. Tat. Tat. I strain to hear outside. Nothing, beyond the tide of traffic on H Street; the chain of the tether ball lifting in the wind, then dropping to lash its pole. Clank clink. Clank clink. At noontime exactly there is a scraping of chairs as we stand to pray the "Angelus" ("The angel of the Lord declared unto Mary . . .").

One hundred miles away, the governor's son was also reciting the "Angelus." Edmund G. Brown, Jr.—Jerry Brown—was a seminarian in Los Altos, studying to become a priest. We saw his picture in the newspaper every year in the Christmas-tree photo from the governor's mansion—a young man with dark eyebrows, dressed in black.

Within twenty years Jerry Brown would assume his father's office. The ex-seminarian expounded upon limits, his creed having shriveled to "small is beautiful," a catchphrase of the sixties. Like John Sutter, Jr., Jerry Brown dismantled his father's huge optimism.

"Here tragedy begins," whispers Sister Mary Regis. "The wheel of fortune creaks downward toward a word buried for centuries in the bed of a stream. . . ."

The Irish nun, an unlikely Rhinemaiden, rehearses the Protestant parable for her fifth-grade class. John Sutter sent one of his men, James Marshall, up to the Sierra foothills to build a sawmill. It was January 1848. In the clear winter stream (here Sister hikes her skirt, shades her eyes with her hand; her eyes seem to scrutinize the linoleum), Marshall spied a glint. "It looked like a lady's brooch."

In the morning, or the next morning, or the next, Sutter dispatched several men to see if they could find more of the stuff. Sutter hoped to keep the discovery secret. But several merchants in the region made it their business to take the news over the hills to San Francisco. And so, within weeks, Sutter's kingdom

—the kingdom intended for John Sutter by the providence of God—was lost in a rush of anarchy. Sutter was abandoned by his men, who would be kings themselves. His herd of cattle, his horses—all were stolen. And his fort—that placid rectangle of dirt in an ocean of grass—his fort was overrun by men who heard the mystical word pronounced out loud.

GOLD.

There were stories. People vaulting from the dentist chair at the approach of my Uncle Raj. "No nigger dentist is going to stick his fingers in my mouth!" There was a price to be paid for living in Sacramento, the dark-green car, the green lawn, the big green house on 45th Street.

My Uncle Raj had three daughters. He wanted a son. I flirted with him. Every Christmas I would ask my Uncle Raj for expensive toys my parents couldn't afford. I wanted a miniature circus. I wanted a cavalry fort.

My uncle called me Coco.

Sutter's son inherited the shambles of his father's dream. John Sutter, Jr., was a tradesman and not a man of the land. John Sutter, Jr., recognized the advantages for trade in situating a new town alongside the river, two miles west of his father's fort. John Sutter, Jr., proposed giving the new river town the old Spanish name for the Valley—Sacramento. Thus Sacramento City flourished while Sutterville—which John Sutter had imagined as teeming, spired, as blessed as Geneva—Sutterville dried up and died.

In my bedroom I sketched visionary plans. A huge aquatic amusement park would parallel the river beneath an animated neon sign of a plunging diver. There would be a riverboat restaurant decked with Christmas lights and a dinner theater. (The movie *Show Boat* had recently been filmed near Sacramento.)

Nothing Lasts a Hundred Years

It was the father's failure Sacramento remembered, not the son's success. John Sutter abandoned his fort, retired to a farm. A short time later he left California for good. His bones are buried in Pennsylvania.

". . . A victim of sudden good fortune," the Irish nun pronounced over him.

Such, too, was Sacramento's assessment of Sutter's life. The town may have owed its combustion to the Gold Rush, but when, within months, the vein of anarchy was exhausted, Sacramento would turn to regard the land itself as representing God's grace. Sacramento became a farm town, the largest in the Central Valley.

Toward the end of August, the air turned foul. Farmers were burning, people said—always this speculation on the cardinal winds—just as people said "peat dust" in March or "hay fever" in May or "alfalfa" in summer.

John Sutter served as a reminder to generations of farmers who lived by the seasons (Low Church lessons of slow growth, deferred reward). For his fall was steep, a lesson suitable to the moral education of generations of flatland teenagers—farm kids who came to Sacramento every August for the State Fair. We would see their pictures in the *Sacramento Bee*, kids from Manteca or Crow's Landing in their starched 4-H uniforms, holding sunflower ribbons over the heads of doomed beasts.

After work, my father and my Uncle Raj drove home together in Raj's new green car—the Mexican and the Indian. They sat in the car with the motor running.

"Go out and bring in your father," my mother would say.

I stole only bits of the story; the rest lay on a shelf too high for me. My Uncle Raj had gotten mixed up in some kind of politics. Once, Uncle Raj had taken my father to "a meeting" in San Francisco.

That was all I knew. That, and I once overheard my mother say on the phone, "We're afraid to have Leo apply for the job. There may be some record."

My father, as everyone knew, would have liked a job at the post office. But he never applied.

Alongside copies of *Life* and *Saturday Evening Post* on the mahogany table in Raj's waiting room were "international" pamphlets.

Was Raj a Communist?

Communists were atheists. Raj was a Catholic. He converted when he married my aunt. He went to mass every Sunday.

One afternoon a dental-supply salesman—his sample case and his hat were in his hand—came out into the waiting room with Raj. It was nearing six o'clock. I sat turning the pages of a magazine. My father was taking down the garbage. I could hear the trash barrel bumping down the stairwell. The man crossed to the table next to me, picked up the stack of pamphlets, and stooped to place them into the waste basket my father had just emptied. "Let's just get rid of these, Dr. Raman." His tone was not friendly but he smiled. "Why look for trouble, I always say," holding out his hand to Uncle Raj. Uncle Raj stared down into the waste basket.

Had my Uncle Raj conspired against paradise?

My uncle's eyes began to cloud at their perimeters. I heard them say he had a heart bother. I heard them say he was worried he might get deported. My uncle had been in some kind of trouble with the Immigration Service. There had been "a trial."

My uncle put an Adlai Stevenson sticker on the back fender of his new green car.

But there were afternoons when my uncle's heart tightened like a fist at the prospect of losing California. In the back room of my uncle's office was a maroon sofa and, over the sofa, a painting of a blond lady being led by a leopard on a leash. Beneath the painting my uncle lay prostrate. At such times my father applied warm towels to the back of my uncle's skull.

Raj had come on ships all the way from Bombay when he was a boy. Now Raj hated the ocean. The swirling ocean was a function of the Immigration and Naturalization Service. The ocean would surely carry him back to India.

What was India, I pondered, but another Mexico. Indians in both places. "Cattle freely roam the streets of Bombay," according to the *World Book Encyclopedia*.

■ ■ ■

My mother remembered Mexico as a girl. She remembered the taste of Mexican ice cream, creamier than here. She remembered walking with her sisters round the plaza at night, the warm Guadalajara nights. She remembered a house—an address—tall shadows against a golden wall. In Mexico her mother made laces to sell, seeming to pluck the patterns out of the air with her fingers—laces fallen, like snowflakes, through time. My mother kept a cellophane bag full of lace in a drawer in the kitchen. She brought the bag out to show us, unfolding the laces tenderly as cobweb. Mexican women are real women, my mother said, caressing the antimacassar spread open upon the table. But the beauty of the lace troubled her. She admitted she never wanted to learn it.

Oh, but my mother's brother Juanito was tall as a tree, strong as a tree, with shade in his eyes. And people threw coins when my mother danced on a table in high-button shoes, tossing her head like a pony at the call of her nickname, Toyita. Toyita, she remembered the lyrics of a song. Ah, there are no love songs like the love songs of Mexico. This country is so dry, like toast, my mother said. Nothing like Mexico, my mother said, lapping the blue milk of the memory of Mexico.

Days of Obligation

My father is a man nearly as old as the century. As a boy he saw Halley's Comet and he gauged his life by the sighting. He said he would live to see the comet's return and now he has surpassed Halley's Comet. My father understands that life is as surprising as it is disappointing. He left Mexico in his late twenties for Australia. He ended up in Sacramento in a white coat, in a white room, surrounded by shelves of grinning false teeth. Irony has no power over my father.

Our last house on "Eye" Street was across from an old cemetery. No memory attached to it. The grass was watered and cut once a month by the city. There were no scrolls or wrought-iron fences; no places to put flowers. There were granite plaques level with the ground. Early dates. Solitary names. Men. Men who had come early to California and died young.

No grandsons or granddaughters came forward in the 1950s when Sacramento needed the land to build a school, a new Sutter Junior High School. A plywood fence was hammered up around the cemetery and, within that discretionary veil, bulldozers chugged and grunted, pulling up moist hairy mounds of what had once been the light of day; trucks came to carry it all away.

In early November, white tule fog rises from the valley floor. My father is easy with this ancient weather reminiscent of the sea. My father is whistling this morning as he scrambles two eggs. My mother turns away from the window, pulling her blue bathrobe closer around her throat. I am sitting at the kitchen table. I am sixteen years old. I am pouring milk onto Sugar Frosted Flakes, watching milk rise in the bowl. My parents will die. I will die. Everyone I know will someday be dead. The blue parakeet my mother has taught to say "pretty boy" swings upon his little trapeze, while my mother pours coffee.

I can no longer remember the cold. In my memory, it is always summer in Sacramento; the apricot tree in the backyard is heavy; the sky is warm and white as a tent.

One summer, my uncle was beautiful. His skin was darker than Mexico. His skin wore shade. It was blue. It was black.

When I was seven years old, my girl cousins threw me into the lake at Lodi and, with several islands to choose from, I swam toward the island of my uncle. His eyes were black and so wide with surprise they reflected the humor of the water. His nipples were blue and wet black fur dripped down his front and floated in the water at his waist.

In the family album, Raj yet lifts me upside down by my legs. I am confident in my abandon as the trees whirl by. My aunt backs away from the camera, regret blurring from her eyes.

"Don't . . . Please. Put him down now, Raj."

Comedy and tragedy merged when I was sixteen. My uncle died.

He was extracting a tooth. He had just begun to tighten the clamp; the water swirled in the expectoral basin (within the patient's skull the awful grating, as of sepulchral stone), when my uncle began to sweat.

"I don't think I'm going to be able to finish. . . ."

The clamp banged down on the metal tray.

The receptionist's scream brought my father from the back lab, still drying his hands with a towel. My father placed the towel under my uncle's head. My father took my uncle's hand, where my uncle lay on the dark-green linoleum; my father easing my uncle down into the ocean.

■　■　■

"Keep me in your prayers," the nun would write years later to her fifth-grade student, remembering him as a boy on her deathbed. Before she died, Sister Mary Regis sent me a card, a confident, florid verse. Inside, she writes she will not be able to come to the lecture I am going to give in Sacramento, as she has a "chronic illness." (She is dying of cancer.)

"Keep me in your prayers, and I do you. Do you remember that you carried a notebook and asked millions of questions?"

The same question: Who is more right—the boy who wanted to be an architect, or his father, who knew that life is disappointment and reversal? (Is the old man's shrug truer than the boy's ambition simply because the shrug comes last?)

■　■　■

In Mexico my father had the freedom of the doves. He summoned the dawn. Each morning at five-thirty, my father would climb the forty steps of the church tower to pull the ropes that loosened the tongues of two fat bells. My father was the village orphan and it was his duty and his love and his mischief to wake the village, to watch it stir: the pious old ladies bending toward mass; the young men off to the fields; the eternal sea.

FOR THE BEST IN PAPERBACKS, LOOK FOR THE 🐧

In every corner of the world, on every subject under the sun, Penguin represents quality and variety—the very best in publishing today.

For complete information about books available from Penguin—including Pelicans, Puffins, Peregrines, and Penguin Classics—and how to order them, write to us at the appropriate address below. Please note that for copyright reasons the selection of books varies from country to country.

In the United Kingdom: For a complete list of books available from Penguin in the U.K., please write to *Dept E.P., Penguin Books Ltd, Harmondsworth, Middlesex, UB7 0DA.*

In the United States: For a complete list of books available from Penguin in the U.S., please write to *Consumer Sales, Penguin USA, P.O. Box 999— Dept. 17109, Bergenfield, New Jersey 07621-0120.* VISA and MasterCard holders call 1-800-253-6476 to order all Penguin titles.

In Canada: For a complete list of books available from Penguin in Canada, please write to *Penguin Books Canada Ltd, 10 Alcorn Avenue, Suite 300, Toronto, Ontario, Canada M4V 3B2.*

In Australia: For a complete list of books available from Penguin in Australia, please write to the *Marketing Department, Penguin Books Ltd, P.O. Box 257, Ringwood, Victoria 3134.*

In New Zealand: For a complete list of books available from Penguin in New Zealand, please write to the *Marketing Department, Penguin Books (NZ) Ltd, Private Bag, Takapuna, Auckland 9.*

In India: For a complete list of books available from Penguin, please write to *Penguin Overseas Ltd, 706 Eros Apartments, 56 Nehru Place, New Delhi, 110019.*

In Holland: For a complete list of books available from Penguin in Holland, please write to *Penguin Books Nederland B.V., Postbus 195, NL-1380AD Weesp, Netherlands.*

In Germany: For a complete list of books available from Penguin, please write to *Penguin Books Ltd, Friedrichstrasse 10-12, D-6000 Frankfurt Main 1, Federal Republic of Germany.*

In Spain: For a complete list of books available from Penguin in Spain, please write to *Longman, Penguin España, Calle San Nicolas 15, E-28013 Madrid, Spain.*

In Japan: For a complete list of books available from Penguin in Japan, please write to *Longman Penguin Japan Co Ltd, Yamaguchi Building, 2-12-9 Kanda Jimbocho, Chiyoda-Ku, Tokyo 101, Japan.*